Christmas Cards
for the Collector

Arthur Blair

B. T. BATSFORD LTD · LONDON

© Arthur Blair 1986

First published 1986

All rights reserved. No part of this publication may
be reproduced, in any form or by any means,
without permission from the Publisher

ISBN 0 7134 5224 2

Typeset and printed by
Butler and Tanner Ltd, Frome and London
for the publishers
B. T. Batsford Ltd
4 Fitzhardinge Street
London W1H OAH

Contents

Acknowledgements

No author ever wrote a book without receiving inspiration from others, and this is part of the pleasure of embarking on the adventure of such writing: meeting interesting people and asking a little assistance on certain points that crop up.

To the following friends the author says thank you for your kindness:

The Royal Librarian, Windsor Castle; Frances Dunkels, Department of Prints and Drawings, British Museum; the President of the Royal Philatelic Society; Jennifer Sweeney, British Telecom Design Unit; The National Philatelic Society; Caroline Eversfield of Rimmel International Public Relations; Stanley Gibbons Gallery; Argyll Etkin Gallery; Maurice Rickards, Chairman of The Ephemera Society; Dorothy Martin, and Rosemary Adcock for her invaluable editorial assistance.

Arthur Blair

Introduction

Anyone deciding to take up the hobby of Christmas card collecting will never regret that decision.

It is a fascinating and rewarding indoor hobby, for it offers plenty of scope for individual expression of one's artistic tastes. The subject is a wide one with a choice of many different sections, each a study on its own with the interesting prospect of building up a collection that, if properly arranged, will be of interest to many friends and in time develop into a display that can be shown to groups of people.

Taking up this pastime is not just a question of gathering together cards of all types and putting them in an album in no special order; the real pleasure is derived from studying the specimens to find out (where possible) the names of the artists, publishers, and writers of the verses. This worthwhile research will increase greatly the pleasure derived from the hobby by giving it a special meaning.

This book sets out to assist the collector of every period, starting from the world's first Christmas card and continuing through the development over the years of these messages of peace and goodwill.

Unlike other hobbies there are at present no annual exhibitions devoted to the collecting of greeting cards; this has been partly due to the attitude of some serious collectors wishing to keep what might be called a low profile as far as their particular interests are concerned. However, through a special exhibition organized by the Ephemera Society which travelled round many towns in the country in 1986, plus month-long shows at Stanley Gibbons's Strand Gallery, the Argyll Etkin showroom in Conduit Street and the British Telecom Headquarters in the City, it was obvious from public reaction that they very much welcomed the innovation of these exhibitions.

Most collectors like to meet or read about fellow enthusiasts and thus keep up-to-date in their collecting, but apart from the few exhibitions mentioned, regular social meetings where collectors talk about their hobby and perhaps exchange specimens are few and far between. However, there is one organization that is developing a greeting card membership – the Ephemera Society – and due credit is given to them on page 125 for their assistance to the author

Although many do not fully realize it, this hobby can offer interesting possibilities for development in a number of sidelines that are important if one wants to explore the history of the hobby in some depth.

This book gives the essential background of greeting cards from 1843 to modern times and how to build up an attractive collection. It should put the new collector on the right road leading to a full enjoyment of the hobby. It is also hoped that collectors already involved in the subject will find in some chapters what might be to them some new thoughts that will enable them to get even greater enjoyment from their collections.

If any reader wants further advice on the subject, he or she can get in touch with me by letter c/o The Ephemera Society.

Here's wishing you all happiness in your collecting.

ONE

How it all began

What inspired a busy man over 140 years ago suddenly to think of his friends at Christmas time with a wish to send them an unusual token of his friendship? And was that whim, which created the world's first Christmas card to unite caring people in messages of peace in December, a sudden idea in a man's mind, or did it really begin 2,000 years ago, when three men wisely travelled through the cold, deep winter to find a Jewish girl in a stable nursing a new born child? We can believe that the gifts and greetings they brought on that first Christmas day still echo down the many years as people send each other a message of peaceful wishes expressed in the form of a simple card commemorating a Baby's birthday.

There was no mysticism in the early events that led to Henry Cole's inspiration that gave the world one of its greatest annual social customs. Christmas and New Year are of course

1. *The beginning of a Christmas card idea: a visiting card with a child's scrap attached to it. The scrap was sometimes stuck on the bottom so the card could be bent forward to show the name of the sender; this would be the reason why early manufactured cards had messages or verses under a partly secured scrap.*

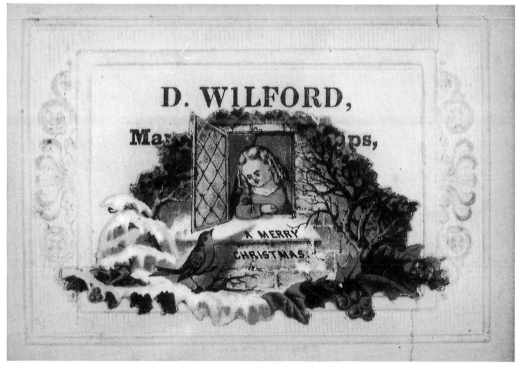

A GUID NEW YEAR

AN' MONY O' THEM

2. Here is a Scottish claim that the first greeting card came from over the border. Charles Drummond, a printer in Leith, Scotland, issued a card showing a jolly fat face with imperfect teeth, but the message 'A Guid New Year an' Mony o' Them' puts this in the category of a New Year card.

closely linked together. Romans in imperial days exchanged small pictures, terracotta lamps, fruit and other such trifles with their friends at the beginning of the year. Such gifts were called *strenae* (from Strenia, the goddess of good health). Some of the heathen activities that took place during the winter solstice were gradually suppressed by the Christian Church. In the British Museum there is a 1467 engraving by 'Master E. S.' showing the Infant Jesus standing on a large flower; a scroll carries a greeting for the New Year: *Ein guot selig ior* (A good and happy year).

The little coloured scraps of many designs that were a product of German printers in the first half of the nineteenth century were often used by adults to convert a visiting card to a Christmas card. A scrap showing a robin, a piece of holly or the words 'Merry Christmas', stuck on a corner of a visiting card, made a seasonal greeting when calling on a friend. These scraps were also used frequently (printed with short loving messages) on early Valentines and on Christmas cards from the 1850s onwards.

The attractively decorated notepaper often available to visitors staying at good-class country and seaside hotels can also be considered a forerunner of the greeting card. Sometimes it was in colour and at Christmas time some visitors to hotels that provided such stationery lost no time in writing to their friends, wishing them the compliments of the season on free decorative notepaper – all good publicity for the hotel.

Further forerunners to be considered are the decorated 'Christmas pieces'. These were usually the province of young people who, to convince parents how skilled they had become from their schooling, wrote in their best hand a greeting for yuletide in the space provided on a special sheet.

To good little children who attended Sunday school regularly, Reward cards were given. These were well printed in colour, usually with a short religious quotation. The youngsters would proudly show them to parents and other members of the family in anticipation of another reward, hopefully in the form of a sixpence. Usually in Scotland it was a silver threepenny piece!

With the addition of a scrap showing a small flower, the inevitable robin or a Christmas wish, these Reward cards were frequently used as greeting cards and it was not long before some publishers used the same designs for Christmas cards.

A claim that Scotland created the first greeting card was put forward by Margaret S. Shinie of Edinburgh, following a statement in a *Naturalist* BBC talk on 5 December 1948 that the first Christmas card was dated 1846. 'The first greeting card was published in 1841 by my grandfather, Charles Drummond, bookseller and printer, of Leith, Edinburgh. The design was a laughing face.'

A number of forerunners of the Christmas card have been briefly mentioned, but there is one very important one that can claim the closest relationship: the Valentine. It seems a little strange that although these messages of devotion, sometimes on parchment in the form of a flat card, were well known in the middle of the eighteenth century, it was not until nearly the middle of the nineteenth century that the first true Christmas card appeared, and when it did publishers were slow to appreciate the commercial possibilities of such greetings; a few years were to elapse before it was realized that the Valentine could be adapted to carry the Christmas message.

3. *The world's second Christmas card, by William Maw Egley. At first it was thought to be the earliest card, since it had a date in the lower right corner that looked like "1842". Egley eventually settled the argument by agreeing that the date was 1848 – the "8" having been mistaken for a "2".*

THE WORLD'S FIRST CHRISTMAS CARD

Henry Cole, born at Bath on 15 July 1808, became one of the greatest English organizers of the nineteenth century. He started work at 15 in the Public Records Office and in time became the assistant keeper there.

Cole was a true lover of art and did a great deal to encourage students to appreciate the finer points of beautiful designs associated with nineteenth-century England. With Richard Redgrave, the painter, he started the publication *Journal of Design and Manufacture* and helped to establish an art shop in London's Old Bond Street (No. 12), calling it Felix Summerly's Home Treasury Office.

In 1851 he was associated with Prince Albert in the promotion of the Great Exhibition. He helped Rowland Hill in the planning of postal reforms, even entering the competition to design the first postage stamp, launched the National Training School for Music, which became the Royal College of Music, and

4. *A boy with a red scarf wishes 'Merry Xmas and a Happy New Year to You'.*

became associated with the plans for the Royal Albert Hall. Through his enthusiasm, and the gift of his collections, it can be claimed that the Victoria and Albert Museum became the first museum of its type in existence.

All these activities made him a very busy man and the story goes that as the month of December of 1843 approached he realized that there would be little opportunity to find leisure time to write his letters of Christmas greetings to his many friends and business associates. It was then that one of his greatest inspirations took shape; an idea that was to become the biggest secular event in the Christmas calendar and in time create a huge industry that has brought wealth to many business concerns and

employment to countless people: the creation of the world's first commercially produced Christmas card.

The story that Cole thought up the idea of a printed card to send to his friends could be true, but it is also possible that he was thinking of his business interest in the shop in Old Bond Street. This shop was his hobby, for through it he endeavoured to educate children and help the general public to appreciate true art as revealed in good design.

Cole lost no time in contacting John Callcott Horsley, a brilliant artist, and within a short while he was shown proofs of a suggested design, which met with his approval. There is little need to describe fully the design, since an original is illustrated here from the writer's collection; but an interesting description of a similar card (sent by the artist to a friend in 1843) was reproduced on a press release sent out by the Post Office in 1975 to publicize the Christmas stamps of that year:

The main picture on the Cole Horsley Card tells us something of life in the 1840s. It shows a picture of eleven people from three generations enjoying a family party. The members of the party are toasting the health of the absent friend, the person who receives the card, in red wine. Only the three smallest children are not holding a glass but are tasting the plum pudding.

Christmas cards played an important part in the lives of Victorians who often stuck them in scrap books and kept them for a lifetime. New cards were often reviewed in the press when they were first published.

The statement in the last sentence of the first paragraph caused the eyebrows of a few observant people to be raised, since the illustration on the Post Office release clearly shows one child in the background draining the contents of a wine glass and another child in the foreground eagerly drinking from a full glass. The design of the card as issued came in for criticism from Victorians who were firmly against indulgence in alcoholic refreshment and demonstrations of passion in public, so they must have been so concerned about the children's welfare that they failed to notice the young couple on the right of the group flirting.

Every year near the month of December articles appear in magazines and newspapers about the Cole–Horsley card, some written with accurate descriptions, others not, but all writers now agree that the card was definitely issued for Christmas 1843. The printing was done on a lithographic stone by Jobbins, Warwick Court, Holborn, London, (1,000 copies) on paperboard cut to 5⅛ × 3¼ inches. They were published by Felix Summerly's Home Treasury Office and sold for one shilling each. In the book *The History of the Christmas Card* by George Buday, published in 1954, the author stated that the cards were hand-coloured by a professional 'colourer' named Mason, and from then on writers on the subject continued to use the colourer's surname only. However, justice was done to him in an article by Olive Tooley in *Country Life* for 19 October 1978 on 'The Work of William Mason (1803–1875)'; but I still wonder how long it took Mr Mason to hand-colour 1,000 copies of a card in many colours.

Inexperienced collectors seeking the very rare card should realize that a facsimile reproduction (Series No. 459) was made in 1884 by De La Rue & Company. Fortunately the fact that it is a reproduction is printed on the back, but if it were stuck down in an album, and as the colouring is quite good, it might be mistaken for an original.

It is believed that there are only 14 Cole–Horsley cards in existence and one of them is an unused specimen. In 1959 the Hallmark Greeting Card Company of Kansas City, USA, heard that there was an unused Cole–Horsley owned by a collector in England, so they sent over one of their representatives, Carrol Alton Means, a well-known collector and researcher, to try to obtain this probably unique item for the Company – he succeeded. It is now in the famous Hallmark Historical Collection, which contains over 40,000 antique cards.

THE DEVELOPMENT

Many factors contributed to the gradual development in the exchange of personal greetings by means of cards at Christmas time. Obviously the improvements made in postal communications contributed to great use being made by the public of the services offered by the General Post Office.

In the struggle for postal reform that took place during the early years of Queen Victoria's reign, one name stands out above all others: Rowland Hill. This ex-schoolmaster became something of an embarrassment to a few important men in the service who, for one reason or another, tried to resist changes in the running of certain departments. Fortunately, the determination of Rowland Hill and his supporters, who were convinced that his ideas made sense, succeeded eventually in overcoming the opposition.

Many authoritative books have been written on the successful development of the Post Office from early Victorian days, and for any reader interested in this fascinating subject a few of the modern books presenting the story in a clear manner are listed in the Bibliography.

The railways and their ever increasing routes across the United Kingdom, also the Travelling Post Office service on many trains, contributed to the build-up of Christmas mail being sent by the public; but an important factor in this trend was the gradual improvement in education for the poorer classes. Illiteracy had been rife among deprived families, where in many cases reading and writing was a blank page. Then it should be remembered that the rates of postage made communications by mail almost impossible for those with a very low wage packet.

When the Treasury was given the authority to change the postage rates and abolish linking rates with the distance a letter was carried, the volume of mail increased. In December 1839 charges were 4d for ½ oz, 8d for 1 oz. In January 1840 rates were reduced to 1d for ½ oz, 2d for 2 oz; in 1871 1d for 1 oz, 1½d for 2 oz; then in 1897 1d for 4 oz, ½d for each additional 2 oz.

The appearance on 6 May 1840 of the

world's first postage stamp, the famous Penny Black, revolutionized letter writing, and when some years later a halfpenny stamp was introduced, the huge quantity of greeting cards in the post became a subject for comment in the newspapers each season.

The 1843 Christmas card had made very little impression on the quantity of mail carried in December that year, and even in the 1850s and '60s cards sent by post were few. However, in the 1870s the 'rush' started and by 1880 the 'flood' began in true fashion.

Before leaving the subject of the first Christmas card and its forerunners, mention should be made of two early envelopes issued before the Cole–Horsley card appeared.

On 13 December 1839 Henry Cole discussed with William Mulready RA, plans for a special pictorial envelope and a letter sheet to be issued at the same time as the Penny Black on 6 May 1840. The design of Britannia sending winged messengers over the ocean to bring the good tidings of worldwide cheap postage received official approval, but when the envelopes went on sale the Press rather unfairly condemned them, and they were soon withdrawn from circulation.

The design was undoubtedly the inspiration for a Christmas card envelope that followed in December 1840. Fores of Piccadilly, London, the dealer in sporting and other prints, commissioned two young artists, Richard and James Doyle, to design a series of comic envelopes, the last one (No. 10) to be for Christmas. An entry in Richard Doyle's diary for 26 November 1840 states:

> Spent the rest of the evening in designing a Christmas envelope which, when done, is to be brought out immediately. There are few things in that way so difficult to design as an envelope, but I think at last we have got one that will do pretty well.

It was a happy design in a style somewhat similar to the 'Mulready', as will be seen from the illustration.

Of the set of envelopes by the Doyles *The Times* had kinder words to say than those used in its criticism of Mr Mulready's design:

> We recommend those who buy post-office envelopes merely for fun – we suppose few purchase them with any other object – to purchase Mr Fores's envelopes instead. They are better and more amusing, both in design and execution, and are certainly more creditable to the public taste.

This envelope, hand-coloured, is a very scarce item, but a collector seeking a genuine example should remember that reproductions, usually uncoloured, were made. In Robson Lowe's *The Encyclopædia of British Empire Postage Stamps* Volume 1 there is a note on these reproductions.

> Imitations of most of these envelopes ... were made from the blocks to illustrate Möens 1893 catalogue. Each can be detected by the name of the lithographer who worked for Möens, F. Deraedemaeker, which is found on each imitation. . . .

[The tiny name is underneath the Punch and Judy man.] J-B. C. Möens was a Belgian dealer who published the world's first philatelic handbook dealing with the falsification of postage stamps.

THE ENVELOPE

Since the envelope played such an important part in the promotion of Christmas cards, a few notes on this useful item of stationery will not be out of place here.

The statement in the *Encyclopaedia Britannica* under 'Paper' that 'Even the common envelope was unknown prior to 1841' does not appear to be correct. According to Frank Staff in an article 'The Envelope. Its Evolution and Development' in *Stamp Lover* for October 1983, the envelope was 'invented' in 1820 by a Mr Brewer, who had a stationers' shop in Brighton. He manufactured these principally for ladies from across the Channel who visited fashionable Brighthelmstone on the South Coast and liked to purchase his fancy, ornamental envelopes, similar to those in vogue on the Continent.

It was perhaps just as well that the greeting

card did not appear a few years before it did, for prior to 1840 the postage on an envelope containing a letter (or card) would have been double. When uniform penny postage was introduced in January 1840, an enclosure, such as a card, would not incur double postage.

Besides being one of the finest printers of postage stamps in existence at the time, the firm of Thomas De La Rue was responsible for many innovations in newspaper printing, and improvements to the quality of playing cards, banknotes and cheques, but we are concerned

here only with their activities associated with the envelope.

Warren, son of Thomas De La Rue, and Edwin Hill, brother of Rowland Hill, joined forces to produce an envelope-cutting machine, which was put into service in the De La Rue works in 1844. In 1851, at the Great Exhibition in London, the firm put on show their invention: a machine that cut the paper, folded and gummed it and within an hour, with but one operator, it produced 2,700 envelopes.

It is believed that the early greeting cards of gentleman's visiting-card size were so produced to allow them to fit into the neat little envelopes produced by the De La Rue envelope-making machine. But a little more research work is needed on this subject to prove that theory.

---

5. *Here is the famous Mulready envelope desired by nearly all philatelists. It was issued from most British Post Offices on 6 May 1840 and is said to have inspired Richard Doyle when he was planning the Christmas envelope.*

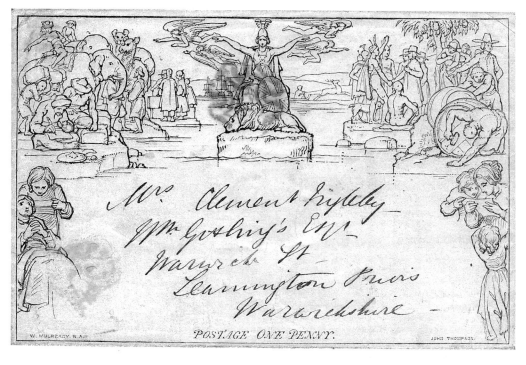

TWO

Animation

Probably the most fascinating type of card is that known as 'animated' in which, by pulling a tassle or a tab, the appearance of the card changes and small designs, flowers or verses are revealed. A brief description of those before me as I write will give some indication of the attraction of these delightful and often surprising items. They are not easy to find in perfect condition due to the fact that inquisitive little Victorian fingers pulled them about quite a lot, and consequently undamaged specimens can be a little expensive.

Here is a particularly fine example which, in a 'resting' position, is a bouquet of many flowers, but when the top cord is pulled the flowers rise up and spread out to uncover a short motto below each flower, and under each motto a tiny picture of happy people taking part in some activity appears. (Early 1870s.)

By pulling a thin silk ribbon on a paper-lace card, a bouquet framed in gold is lowered, and three little angels disappear to reveal the greeting, 'Happy Christmas to my Friend.'

A downward pull on a tab changes a card of flowers into four tiny platforms on which children stand and pull up a frame behind which is 'A Merry Christmas' and greetings behind each child.

Animation transforms another bouquet of flowers into a pretty wedding scene with children. The decorative border is in gold and the card perforated all round the edges.

Christmas and New Year greetings appear behind six separated flowers when a red ribbon is pulled and it also reveals a picture of people and children taking part in many activities near a house with a boating lake and a small bridge from which children are fishing. It is surprising how the artists of these colourful scenes could condense such perfect little pictures into such little space.

Gold borders and oval frames surround small bunches of flowers, which disappear when a lower tab is pulled to uncover 'A very merry Xmastide' and other seasonal good wishes. Another edition of the same card has, instead of the flowers, pictures depicting a toast to a couple at a dinner table, a girl reading a letter, a young man offering a gift to his lady-love, and a girl helping another with her wedding veil.

With another tab card the little windows with flowers encircling children are opened by one's finger to show more children in active occupations, and when the tabs are pulled up, and also down, four separate greetings appear.

Another card to pull is in fact five cards in one. Tabs appear on all sides of the main card and, when these are pulled, another card slides out. Again the pictures are very pretty: a girl carrying a garland on what appears to be a garden rake; on the other cards, children among flowers. Although there is no publisher's imprint shown, one card has a young girl in a white dress with a dove on her hand, the same design as used on a two-panel card with an imprint 'Marcus Ward & Co.' Not many of these five-in-one types have survived

6. *When the silk ribbon is pulled on this paper-lace card two doves, each on a panel, emerge and move aside, and two little girls with a cupid above present themselves and a message below.*

7. *The small envelope supported by cherubs contains the message 'A Merry Christmas'.*

inn on which are the words, 'A Merrie Xmas to Ye'. People in Shakespearian costume are entering the inn shown on the front cover and, when this is raised, on the other side of it a group of seven adults and four children pop up, the latter being given refreshments from a table. Behind them, when the side-panels are moved back, people are seen sitting round the well-appointed room with a large fire in the grate; three musicians are providing music in a corner while a man, presumably Shakespeare himself, is sitting in an armchair, talking to a little girl.

A children's party with many guests is the happy view when the two panels of another card are opened. The front shows the youngsters arriving by carriage and entering the house, while a boy road-sweeper clears a path in the snow, and a man carries a sandwich board announcing a Christmas pantomime. A paper-lace border frames this delightful picture.

The exterior of a theatre is another happy scene. 'Ye Christmas Pantomime' is above the three entrances through which the elegantly dressed audience is moving. It must be an important occasion for the carriages that have arrived each have two red-coated footmen standing at the rear of the vehicles, while a large crowd of onlookers stand in the foreground. A discreet little advertisement for Benjamin Sulman who produced the card is on a small billboard on the back of a man: 'B. Sulman Christmas Cards' it announces. When the two exterior panels are opened the stage is raised up to show the players in action; on the left and right are boxes crowded with people.

These tableaux are fascinating peep-shows and no collection can be considered complete without them; but they need looking after as they can be damaged if carelessly handled, so be on the alert when showing them to children!

MECHANICALS

Closely associated with the animated and the tab cards is the mechanical type. By gently manipulating a part of the card, it is transformed into a kind of toy model.

because the very nature of their pull-out novelties led to the destruction of many of them at the hands of over-enthusiastic youngsters.

TABLEAUX

Like the animated and the tab cards, the tableau variety attracted a lot of attention when they appeared in the 1880s, and they are still regarded as an exciting item that most collectors are pleased to own. Although they are not very scarce they fetch good prices when in good condition.

One tableau depicts a large snow-covered

8. *These excited children are looking at a Punch and Judy show on a 'stand-up' card. By pulling the front back the audience is moved some distance from the 'stage'. A small pasteboard lever at the back supports the card.*

These 'trick' cards were folded flat so that they could be inserted into an envelope for protection during their journey to a friend. When the simple 'mechanics' were operated – in other words, gently pulled into action by hand – they would stand up on their own, so they were much appreciated by people decorating a mantelpiece, a piano or a small table, to make a room look festive for Christmas.

Because of the amount of work that went into the manufacture of these enchanting cards, many of which could produce a three- and four-dimensional effect, they were more expensive to produce than the 'normal' varieties. But although they were quite popular with people who could afford them, publishers such as Marcus Ward, Thomas De La Rue and Louis Prang of America had no time for them since they considered that cards should be of the finest design, with no 'tricks' or novelties.

Many of these cards do not have the name of the publisher on them. They are well produced and their mechanical motivation often relies on leverage activated by thread, ribbon, and short narrow strips of thin pasteboard. Some cheap folded cards were produced, having flowers on the outside and, inside, scraps of a girl on the left, a boy on the right, both surrounded by flowers. When the card is opened folded strips on the back of the couple move them forward. (Dated 1889.)

The seventeenth-century story of Punch and Judy, created by an Italian comedy actor named Silvio Fionillo, is being acted on a semi-glossy card, watched by four excited children who move back from the scene when the front of the card is pulled back. Two folded pieces of pasteboard create the distance between 'stage' and 'audience'. There is a support at the back to enable the whole scene to stand up.

A lyre covered in forget-me-nots is the main background to a lovely little picture which displays pink paper roses that open up when a strip of card at the back slides along the strings of the lyre and the roses reveal the greeting, 'Wishing you a Happy Christmas.'

Many of these cards have a religious motif and were treasured by young and old people alike. Normally they were not pasted in albums, which would have affected the moving mechanism, but were carefully preserved with other mementoes of happy times; for this reason a number of specimens in good condition are available to the collector today.

An impressive card is one with a radiating star of many colours stuck on at the top; when a silk ribbon is pulled three guardian angels move forward in their clouds to gaze down at a baby asleep. The angels in their long white gowns have their wings glistening in sprinkled frost. A sliding hinge at the back enables this picture to stand up and it would have been a lovely little scene when placed near a subdued light in a Victorian room.

To end these short descriptions of a few 'action' cards, one particular type that most collectors seek is a thick double card on the front of which an embossed cornucopia of forget-me-nots is shown, below this in gold, 'May Christmas bring you Happiness'. The card opens downwards to show a lovely panorama; from a sky-blue background trees stand and from these an angel appears, bearing a cornucopia of roses. In front of her is a strip of muslin sprinkled with little flowers and a handsome couple in elegant eighteenth-century costume. In front of them there is a silvery pond surrounded by flowers and in front of this five separate groups of small blooms come into view. The sentiment at the base reads:

> If the direction of affairs
>   Depended but on me,
> What gay and downright happy times
>   This Season you should see!

The credit initials E.E.G. stand for E. E. Griffin, who worked for Wolff Hagelberg of Berlin, whose representative in London was Ernest Falck & Co. (1869.)

For people fortunate enough to have a glass cabinet containing small objects of Victoriana, a few of the above-mentioned cards placed at the back of the cabinet make a perfect background for the other objects displayed. It is a comforting and perhaps sentimental thought that such elegant cards with all their associations with many, many years gone by can still give pleasure to the present generation.

THREE

The language of flowers

O, my love's like a red, red rose,
   That's newly sprung in June;
O, my love's like the melodie
   That's sweetly play'd in tune.

Burns

One of the loveliest subjects it is possible to build up in a collection is that devoted to flowers, and since flora as a design for cards has been popular from the early days, hundreds of different blooms, from a simple daisy to an exotic lily, are available for the enthusiast to form an outstanding display of beauty.

Mounted on black or white album pages ($9\frac{1}{2} \times 11$ inches) with a brief description under each flower (two large cards or four smaller ones to a page) the display cannot fail to charm everyone who views it.

If you are lucky enough to find a copy of

the book *The Illuminated Language of Flowers*, with illustrations in colour by Kate Greenaway and text by Jean Marsh, co-creator and star of the famous television series *Upstairs, Downstairs*, you will see that it lists 700 flowers and their meanings.

Another very detailed book *Flowers and Flower Lore* by the Reverend Hilderic Friend is a work that years ago writers on the subject consulted in order to get their facts right on the meaning of legends, etc. If an interested person can trace a copy in a second-hand book-shop, fortune is smiling on that searcher, for a second edition of the Reverend's volume was published in London by W. Swan Son-nenschein and Co. in 1884 – and is rare.

In Queen Victoria's time secrecy between sweethearts was sometimes a necessity – due to the strictness of certain parents who tried to

9. *'Where shines the King – the Flower of flowers – The great – the one true Christmas Rose!' So ends the short poem by Francis Davis on this card with its delicate white blossoms – a Marcus Ward production.*

keep their daughters locked away (in a sense) until the right man came along, preferably with a golden key. But in those so-called good old days lovers were able to communicate secretly through the medium of flowers. The fact that Papa might intercept the small bouquet and, with the aid of *Old Moore's Almanac*, translate the message behind the floral communication was a risk that had to be taken by the young lovers.

The suggestion that messages could be clearly expressed in a bunch of flowers is no figure of imagination; it is also a fact that flowers on Christmas cards were often chosen by romantic folk because of the meaning associated with each flower. However, in the many floral cards issued today the language of flowers has little significance, yet no one is so dull as not to appreciate the meaning behind a dozen red roses.

Cards to look for include those that name the flower shown. Some modern cards give interesting details on the back of or inside the card of the blooms depicted.

10. *This is a large embossed card of red roses, elegantly arranged to fill the wide area.*

The most popular flower is the rose. It has a beauty that only a poet can describe, a perfume that has not yet been destroyed by over-development, and for all varieties only one recognized meaning – love.

While the majority of roses depicted on cards are red, since that brilliant colour catches the eye so readily, the delicate white of the Christmas rose is certainly 'a thing of beauty [and] a joy forever'. A neat little card by Marcus Ward & Co. has a verse that likens this particular flower to the Christ Child. The meaning of this rose is 'Relieve my anxiety'.

In a move to improve designs of mass-produced cards, in 1880 Louis Prang of America organized a competition with cash prizes to find artists capable of producing designs that would improve the image of the trade in such commodities. It was not just a case of creating

1877
CHRISTMAS TIDE

a pretty drawing: to be successful an artist had to appreciate some of the technical difficulties in the printing of this type of semi-specialized work. The competition resulted in several fine designs being submitted by artists, many of whom were inspired by the possibility of monetary gain. The final result was that Louis Prang published many new cards that further increased this firm's good reputation.

Not to be outdone by the American firm's enterprise, some English publishers also organized a somewhat similar contest, and again the result brought forth many fresh designs onto the market. One of the top prize designs issued by Siegmund Hildesheimer & Co. showed white roses and buds with a background of

Flower cards are not without variety in styles. An attractive one has an embossed envelope with a pale mauve card, a gold frame pasted on the 'address' side and a floral scrap secured to an oval of black velvet framed in gold. The back of the envelope has its flaps sealed with a small scrap of flowers. When the evelope is opened by folding back the flaps

11. A sedate party takes place on Eugène Rimmel's Christmas Tide greeting for 1877, perfumer by Appointment to HRH the Princess of Wales – dated 1873.

there is usually a card inside with a picture and verse on it, or a perfumed sachet. These are not easy to find.

To give some idea of how a swain could convey his feelings to a maiden without committing himself in writing, which could have dire consequences should he be ungallant enough to change his affection, here are a few of the meanings in the language of flowers:

Anemone (garden)	Forsaken
Bluebell	Constancy
Buttercup	Childishness
Carnation, striped	Refusal
Chrysanthemum, red	I love
yellow	Love ignored
white	Truth
Clematis	Mental beauty

Clover	Be mine
Columbine, red	Trembling with anxiety
Crocus, spring	Youthful gladness
Cyclamen	Diffidence
Daffodil	Regard
Daisy, wild	I will think of it
Fern	Fascination
Fleur-de-Lis	Flame, I burn
Forget-me-not	True love
Foxglove	Insincerity
French Marigold	Jealousy
Fuchsia, scarlet	Taste
Geranium, scarlet	Comforting, stupidity
Hollyhock	Ambition
Honeysuckle	Generous and devoted affection
Hyacinth, white	Unobtrusive loveliness
Iris	Message
Ivy	Marriage
Lavender	Distrust
Lilac, purple	First emotions of love
white	Youthful innocence
Lily, white	Purity
yellow	Falsehood, gaiety
Lily of the Valley	Return of happiness
London Pride	Frivolity
Marigold	Despair
Narcissus	Egotism
Nasturtium	Patriotism
Orange Blossom	Your purity equals your loveliness
Pansy	Cuddle-me-to-you
Pink Carnation	Woman's love
Polyanthus	Pride of riches
Poppy, red	Consolation
Primrose	Early youth
Rosebud, Moss	Pure and lovely
Rosemary	Remembrance
Shamrock	Lightheartedness
Snapdragon	Presumption
Snowdrop	Hope
Star of Bethlehem	Purity
Stock	Lasting beauty
Sunflower, tall	Haughtiness
Sweet Pea	Delicate pleasures, Departure
Sweet William	Gallantry
Thistle, Scotch	Retaliation
Thrift	Sympathy
Tulip	Fame
Violet, blue	Faithfulness
Wallflower	Fidelity in adversity
Water Lily	Purity of heart

PERFUMED SACHETS

In the 1860s and '70s perfumed sachets in the form of a Christmas or New Year card became a great favourite with the ladies who were particularly pleased when they were presented with them by their menfolk.

These sachets were very elegant, often made up of gold paper-lace or silk, showing bouquets of flowers when the front flaps on some varieties were opened. They were padded with tissue paper or cotton wool to which a few drops of perfume had been added.

The firm usually associated with these fragrant cards was Rimmel; their name with the 1860 address usually appeared on a wafer seal, 'E. Rimmel, 96 Strand, London', which closed the flaps of the envelope enclosing the sachet.

A few words about the famous perfumers will enable the collector to appreciate why the idea of these Christmas sachets developed into a vogue among the ladies.

Monsieur Rimmel was a pupil of Monsieur Lubin, perfumer to Napoleon's Empress Josephine. He eventually came to England and late in the 1820s took over a Bond Street perfumery. In 1834 his son Eugene joined his father in the London business.

The family owned a large flower farm in the South of France and, with skilful cultivation and blending, the many fragrances produced were bottled and sold to wealthy people and royalty. Eugene Rimmel was a great believer in the power of skilled advertising and at the Great Exhibition of 1851 he built a perfume fountain that spread its fragrance throughout the hall; he also designed a perfume steam vaporizer which was introduced into some hospitals. He founded the French Hospital in London and was awarded the coveted Legion of Honour.

Eugene died in 1887 and, although his sons took over the business, it began to go down

With the Season's Greeting.

12. *A large scrap of Father Christmas rushing off on his sledge to deliver toys is the centre piece on this thick, green tinted card. The surrounding dried grasses, fern and flowers add to the charm of this novel card.*

hill. Eventually it regained its popularity and in 1949 it was taken over by Robert Calpin and his sister Rose. Today Rimmel International Ltd is one of the biggest names in the cosmetic business.

Rimmel's sachets cost retailers from 6d to half-a-guinea each, a price governed by the style and the amount of work put into their making.

A few other firms produced perfumed cards, some of which had simply a small greeting on the front or a poem with a scrap added as simple decoration, such as one issued by Marcus Ward & Co. in 1876, filled with powder.

Apart from the many small almanacs Rimmel produced in the 1870s, the firm also issued Christmas cards and, through the kindness of their Public Relations Officer, Caroline Eversfield, I was able to examine all the objects and ephemera in their archives. The firm keeps up

the spirit of the season by producing each year special Christmas cards which are reproductions of very early perfumed cards and almanacs.

DRIED GRASSES AND FLOWERS

Picture, if you will, long trestle tables placed end-to-end in a factory room with bare floorboards. Seated at the trestles are women perhaps airing their views on husbands and children, working conditions and wages. Their hands are as busy as their tongues.

Beside each worker is a box of greeting cards and in front of them small bundles of short, dried grasses, tiny flowers and ferns. They select a card, pick up a sprig of heather or shamrock, bleached grass and a little flower and perhaps a piece of fern, and deftly secure them by means of an adhesive to an appropriate position on the card's design. Thus these women created objects that brought a vague sense of nature to the receivers of such novelties.

As the additions to the cards could be damaged if handled carelessly they were treated with some respect; because of this many still

RIMMEL'S FLOWER FARM AT NICE circ. 1860

repose in old albums, their tiny grasses and flowers unaffected by the 100-year-long confinement between pages.

Because these embellishments were rather fragile they are often found damaged and if in this state one should hesitate before buying them; but of course if they have been acquired through the family or as a gift from a friend, then they should be kept as an example of this type of greeting.

Ireland issued some cards on which sprigs of real shamrock formed a neat picture of a harp, with a message in Irish Gaelic 'A Pleasant Christmas: Shamrocks from Ireland.'

A very scarce English card on heavy board with a pale green background and gilt edges has a large scrap of Santa Claus riding on his toy-filled sledge; round the sides and base of the scrap is a fascinating variety of natural grasses, little flowers and 'With the Season's Greetings' in gilt lettering.

In many old scrapbooks there are often two or three examples of the manufactured type of cards just mentioned, but in addition to these there is always the chance of finding one that was home-made entirely of ferns and grasses, etc., that had been gathered, dried and cut to shape and expertly arranged to form a pattern. These are to be treasured even more than the manufactured card because not only are they unique – a genuine 'one off' – but sentimentally they reveal the love of someone who painstakingly created them for a special friend.

Because of labour costs these dried fern and flower cards are a thing of the past – with probably one exception: neat single cards that for many years have been sold in shops devoted to religious books, pictures and kindred subjects. They usually have scalloped edges

15. *Large daisies with a 'floating' butterfly (attached to the card by a paper mount); particularly attractive because some of the flowers extend outside the card's surface.*

13. *A perfumed sachet, the front flaps of which open up to show an attractive arrangement of flowers.*

14. *The fragrant flower farm of Rimmel's at Nice, where grew many flowers that supplied the perfume for My Lady's sachet. A season's greeting for the 1860s.*

and wording on the front such as 'Merry Christmas, Greetings from the Holy Land' and a dried fern arranged in the shape of a small tree with petals in various colours pasted on the ends of the branches and a little flower on the base; below this 'Flowers from the Holy Land'. On the reverse appears a shooting star and another message 'With all good wishes for a Merry Christmas and a Happy New Year'; below this: 'Made in Jordan'.

One of these little cards makes a fitting end piece to the section on dried grasses and flowers.

GLORIA IN EXCELSIS DEO

Flowers from Bethlehem ✚ Fleurs de Bethléem
Fiori di Betlemme ✚ Blumen v. Bethlehem

16. *Flowers from Bethlehem form a bower for the
Baby Jesus on this card from the Holy Land. The
flowers are, naturally, small and dried. These neat
souvenirs can be obtained today from many shops
selling religious books and articles.*

17. *Children and flowers are the two most popular
subjects on cards. Two little girls gather flowers on
this tiny card by Marcus Ward of the 1870s.*

MAY CHRISTMAS BRING THEE MANY JOYS!

CHILDREN

Christmas belongs to children – Santa Claus,
the robin, crackers, the fir tree, the Baby Jesus
in his crib, the plum pudding, the parties and
even the snow.

All these things are part of a child's dream,
part of the world of make-believe that must
come true. There is no happiness where there is
no laughter of young folk, their little squabbles,
their demand for toys and more toys, all of
which makes the older folk feel young again
when they remember their own faraway child-
hood, the fun in the games they had and, of
course, the tears that vanished into joy when
everything suddenly went right.

All these things are quietly mirrored in gaily
coloured Christmas cards specially created for
children, and they go back in time to the
earliest days when greetings recovered from
the silence that followed the first card of all.

In the 1860s cards were small and delight-
fully juvenile, but they usually conveyed the
message that 25 December was Children's
Day. It is a delight to look through a collection
devoted to children, for there is simplicity,
humour and often a party-spirit running
through most designs with an occasional feeling of pity when an urchin with bare feet and
threadbare clothes is shown standing in the
snow hoping for a crust or a small coin.

The children on the early cards are nearly
all well-dressed and when out of doors in the
winter season the girls usually wear plenty of
clothing, nearly always hats or bonnets, elastic-
sided or button-up boots, heavy stockings and
sometimes a muff.

It might be of interest for those looking out
for cards that are becoming scarce to have
brief details of some good designs and their
publishers. A number of them came from an
1860s-'70s scrap book and are of the visiting
card size, such as one of Marcus Ward & Co.,
showing two little girls gathering flowers on a
coloured picture $1\frac{5}{8} \times 8\frac{1}{8}$ inches pasted on a pale
green card $3\frac{1}{4} \times 1\frac{7}{8}$ inches. The message is 'May
Christmas bring Many Joys.'

Another card, slightly larger, has a bevelled
edge picture of two beautifully dressed girls

18. *Two well-dressed little girls watch an equally well-dressed boy in a velvet suit playing with a dove.*

19. *A boy and a girl are skating happily on the ice, oblivious of the nearby danger sign.*

20. *Here a gallant boy is teaching a girl to roller skate.*

watching a boy in an elegant brown velvet suit with a white collar talking to a dove on his hand; by moving the picture forward a three-dimensional scene opens up showing children playing, behind them are ducks on a pond; the separate background has the greeting on a garland of roses. This is an early animated card. Two young skaters on a white scallop-edged card are so engrossed with each other that they are uncomfortably near ice that is cracking up and showing a sign DANGER-OUS. Under the girl's foot is 'A Happy Christmas to You', but it won't be for them unless they look where they are going.

Benjamin Sulman, London, in the 1860s produced decorated envelopes, notepaper, sachets and cards. These are interesting items to acquire not so much because of the early date of manufacture, but for reasons of attractive designing, such as a card $2\frac{3}{4} \times 3\frac{3}{4}$ inches showing a small boy teaching a dainty Miss to roller skate. The colours of their dress are

enhanced by the solid gold background.

A few writers of articles on early Christmas cards state that religious designs are not very frequently seen on these cards. This surmise has no foundation at all. Although flowers and birds might come near to the 'top of the charts', religion is not all that far down on the list. An example of an early religious card for children has Baby Jesus in a crib with two young angels beside him and in the background a candlelit tree heavy with toys and framed by holly and ivy.

A little girl – it might be a boy, since they sometimes dressed alike in those days – is vigorously waving a Union Jack on a card dated 1877, published by Joseph Mansell, London, quite an early appearance of this flag on a Christmas card. The design is enclosed by holly and flowers with a gold background.

Two little girls in blue and red dresses respectively and white bonnets are playing a game that is 2,000 years old – Battledore and Shuttlecock. Green grass and a gold sky is the background to this Marcus Ward greeting.

The initials 'H & F' on this next card mean that it was published by Hildesheimer & Faulkner, London. The design has three young women in a punt picking blossom from a tree on a small island on the river.

'Christmas Gladden Thy Heart With Faithful Friends' is the sentiment on a card by Siegmund Hildesheimer & Co., London and New York. It has a boy in a very pale green suit and red stockings reclining on a couch feeding his small dog with a biscuit. Dated 1885, the series number is 478, which might be of interest to anyone studying the fine production of this firm operating from 1876 to the 1890s. Another of their attractive cards has a child wearing a blue and white outfit with a large pink sash. She holds a box of coloured candies. The card is designed to represent a tambourine. Printed in Germany, serial No. 997.

A large card of an attractive shape also published by the above firm, designed in England

21. *Two angels worship the Christ Child in front of a well-lighted and decorated tree.*

With best wishes
for Christmas.

22. *This is a much larger card, showing two children
leaning over the window-sill and kissing under the
mistletoe with five robins watching.*

MAY CHRISTMAS BRING YOU MANY JOYS!

23. Battledore and Shuttlecock is the game between these two youngsters. A Marcus Ward greeting.

Wishing you a very happy Christmas.

24. The popular sailor suit and cap or hat made many an appearance on cards of the Victorian and the Edwardian times.

WITH THE SEASON'S GREETINGS

25. Raphael Tuck's card shows six not very active children doing nothing in particular.

26. *Two children sing a goodnight song 'Blessing to You and Yours' on this charming card by Ernest Nister & Co.*

and printed in Germany, serial No. 1019, shows two youngsters by a snow-covered windowsill kissing under the mistletoe, while five interested robins watch them from red-berried branches. (Artistic licence, here – not the children kissing, for that is normal at Christmastime, but the appearance of five robins together, for it is said that you never see more than two of these birds near each other).

An interesting study can be made of the various styles of the sailor suit for boys. A number of well-known publishers issued cards depicting this form of uniform so popular during Victorian, Edwardian and Georgian times.

Raphael Tuck & Sons contributed many delightful items to the children's gallery. There is a picture of six rather stiff youngsters in party dress sitting and standing about as if they were waiting for the flash of the photographer's powder.

A lovely card, also by Tuck, has a scantily clad fairy-like child sitting on the leaves of flowers, looking in alarm at a huge wasp that has just alighted on a large leaf in front of the child. The message strikes a more peaceful note 'Over the mountains, and cities and dells, Ring Christmas Peace and Joy – Oh Bells!'

Let us end these random thoughts on greetings for children by noting one that is appropriate for the occasion. It was published by Ernest Nister & Co., London, (1880s–90s), and printed in Bavaria. It offers 'Christmas Blessings to You and Yours' and shows a little girl and a boy singing together from a song-sheet. 'Blessed are the pure in heart for they shall see God.'

—FOUR—

Elegance

SILK FRINGES

Single and double (folded) cards with silk fringes right round the edges appeared at the beginning of the 1880s. They were more expensive than the unadorned cards and appealed to those looking for something unusual in a pretty-pretty way. The colours of the silk fringes were bright, and as some of the early folded ones were sometimes a little awkward to open, a cord and tassel were added on one or both sides to overcome this very slight problem.

Flowers – the rose, pansy, primrose, forget-me-not and violet – were the most popular subject for the designs, though sailing boats sometimes made an appearance. A few flowers, such as the red rose, were heavily embossed and they look quite beautiful. One variation in style is a large specimen displaying three gilt-edged cards of violets; the satin front is heavily padded with one corner turned back to show small embroidered flowers, under which is the word 'Souvenir'.

The large single cards with silk fringes are considered by many collectors to be among the most attractive Christmas greetings of all; their sizes vary from an 8-inch square to $9\frac{1}{2} \times 7\frac{1}{4}$ inches. The first of four specimens before me as I write shows a Nativity scene placed as a large picture above a wide fireplace with a blazing fire in the grate and a long bowl of greenery on the mantelpiece. The second card has two superbly coloured birds on a pink rose bush. The third has an elegant, well-dressed lady changing her shoes outside her front door, having been out shopping on the snow-covered pavements, and the fourth is a pleasing Santa

Claus framed in a laurel of holly, with 'Merry Christmas' written above his fur hat. This particular card has a design on the back of rabbits searching for food in a woodland scene, while two owls look down at them from a snow-covered card that wishes everyone 'A Merry Christmas'. Round the gold frame are the designers' names: Walter Satterlee and Susie B. Skelding and above these 'Copyright 1883 White, Stokes & Allen'.

A few children's Christmas and New Year cards were also embellished with silk fringes in various colours. A most attractive set shows the heads and shoulders of very bonny youngsters. They were also issued without the fringe.

Although the word 'copyright' appears on some of these 'frillies' – as they were someimes called – that must have referred to the design only and not the novelty of the adornment, for firms such as Raphael Tuck, Hildesheimer, Thomas Stevens (at their Stevengraph factory in Coventry), Marcus Ward and Louis Prang of Roxbury, USA (who produced some oustanding examples of these cards), appear to have thought up this novelty at the same time, due either to whispers in the trade or great commercial minds thinking alike.

CORD AND RIBBON

The greeting card started its existence as a single illustrated piece of rectangular pasteboard, and it remained in a horizontal or vertical flat shape for many years.

When the folded cards appeared they were without insets, but eventually these were added to make the product more impressive-

looking by having the greeting and a verse, or even an extra illustration, on the additional folded leaves. But these had to be secured in the card, especially when the insets consisted of four, eight or perhaps twelve pages. This problem was easily solved by a coloured cord, often with a tassel, tied round the spine of the card and the extra pages.

In the 1890s coloured silk ribbons began to replace cords and in 1899–1900 the ribbon, instead of going round the card's fold, went through two holes on the left side of the card and was tied in a bow. Some very fine flower cards in this style were issued by Raphael Tuck; they were most attractively shaped.

27. *A beautiful lady comes in out of the cold on this very attractive card of the 1880s. These silk-fringed varieties could cost about 10/– (50p) or $3, which was quite a good price in those days.*

28. *The head and whiskers of Santa Claus is in a garland of holly on this 8 in square 'Merry Xmas' greeting. The wide fringe is white, setting off the green and bright red of the berries. This is a flat card, but there were smaller folded ones with a cord attached to make it easier to open; there were usually pictures on all four sides.*

'The Season's Souvenir' was the title of a card in the form of a booklet that had to have a securing ribbon through two holes. It was quite an expensive item that for many became a treasured possession. It consisted of 12 gold-edged pages. Its front cover shows a girl on a bridge beside a mill, waving goodbye to her man; the other side of the cover has the same farewell scene viewed from the front. On page three the man has turned round to wave back at the girl and on the fourth page a story of gentle love is told in verse, and so on through each page, some of them partly cut out to show the scene to come as the journey unfolds in picture and verse, ending with:

And should e'er a shadow loom
On your path, be its foretelling
But of greater joy that follows,
While around your soul's fair dwelling,
In the hidden nooks and hollows
That the heart must seek for resting,
May the bird whose name is Peace
Find a chosen place for nesting,
Where its song shall never cease.

The poem was by Helen Maud Waithman; the publishers were Ernest Nister & Company of London (1880s–90s) and E. Dutton & Company of New York. The printing was done at the Nister works in Nuremberg (Bavaria).

29. *For the early folded card with an inset a cord was required to keep the inset intact; this was usually of coloured silk with a tassel, an added attraction to a greeting.*

30. *Silk ribbon began to take the place of cord in the 1890s, usually placed round the card's fold. Then at the end of the century the ribbon went through two holes on the left of the card and ended in a neat bow.*

The Season's Souvenir.

A Poem
by
Helen Maud Waithman

London:
Ernest Nister
24 St Bride Street E.C.

New York:
E.P. Dutton & Cº
31 West Twenty Third Street

Printed by E. Nister at Nuremberg (Bavaria.)

31. *A delightful souvenir of the season of goodwill, this gold-edged 12-page booklet (5¾ in × 4 in) was more of a Christmas present than a card. The poignant story is told in pictures, and in a poem by Helen Maud Waithman, published jointly by Ernest Nister, London and E. P. Dutton, New York. It was printed on thick card at Nuremberg, Bavaria.*

In the early part of the twentieth century, cards with embossed celluloid covers in bright colours made their appearance. The method of securing the cover to the inside leaves was usually by cord and tassel, but in some of the cheaper varieties the cover was secured by machine stitching. These cards were popular with less affluent people, but it was said that because of the inflammable covers they gradually fell out of favour. In those early days, cards were often tied on Christmas trees as additional decorations and as trees were sometimes lit up by small candles, the danger of a celluloid card coming in contact with a lighted candle and flaring up was always a risk.

Apart from silk plush and satin finish cards with floral designs that attracted good sales in the 1870s and '80s, a number of them by Raphael Tuck, there is a special type of card that has novelty and artistry combined in its make-up. These greetings are sometimes overlooked by collectors searching for florid varieties, but by giving a closer look at the less ornate cards many a gem of a design can be found.

Here are a few brief notes on the neat cards that were favoured by some people who liked to send their friends greetings that were 'genteel' in their artistic appearance.

First, a thick card 2⅞ inches square with a miniscule embroidered design on satin of a country scene (cottage, trees, pond and a cart) on an almost oval shape enclosed by a thin cord. Surmounting this are birds and flowers and underneath 'A Gladsome Christmas to You', all in silver.

A yacht is the central design of a larger card, also printed in silver, with a pale blue background with many seagulls and a crescent

32. (left) *This handshake within a horseshoe on a celluloid card hopes the recipient will have 'Good Luck Which Ever Way You Go.' The covers of these cards were quite inflammable and it is believed that this caused them to lose their popularity with those who liked a somewhat gaudy greeting.*

33. (below) *The attraction of this sea picture is that the yacht has on its main sail a coloured picture of another yacht apparently embroidered in satin.*

34. (right) *This small square card (2⅝ in) at first glance might look slightly insignificant, but a closer look at the original discloses that it has the appearance of a delicately embroidered picture of the countryside on a palette-shaped frame enveloped in a thin cord.*

moon. But the delightful thing about this is that the aft sail carries a lovely little picture embroidered in colours on satin.

Two delightful collie dogs appear in a small silk frame on a card with pink roses, a gold Christmas message and the edges of the card roughly scalloped.

Another neat card has a printed country scene that is typically Victorian: a church in the background and trees in the foreground. This is framed in an arch of large bricks, and perched on branches outside the little picture are two brown owls.

Pink, red, cerise and white silk flowers surround another tiny framed design of a distant country house with tall trees and a wide brook. 'Joyous be thy Christmas' is the greeting on this pretty 4-inch square, bevel-edged card.

Another dainty card has pale and deep mauve silk violets and leaves spread across an open fan, below which is the verse:

Christmas!
Bright thoughts come not at call,
In our inner hearts they spring,
May Christmas bring you all
That Health, Love and Peace
Conjoined can bring.

The back of an imitation envelope was quite a favourite background for a number of early cards, sometimes with made-up postal markings. One such envelope-type has brightly coloured silk flowers and opening buds across the flap of the envelope.

One particular all-over silk card is in an unusual form: the front cover has a picture of a small church set among trees reflected in the water. The front folds back to show another silk card with a ribbon and bow that secures four pages inside with the greeting, the sender's name and a verse by Clifton Bingham (1880).

All these cards I have examined are of the flat type, except for the one last mentioned. Few have the name of their publishers printed on them.

PANELS

A type of card that was in vogue from about 1875 to 1885, due to its novelty combined with good design, was the panel or triptych in the form of a little screen. There were two-panel, triptych (three tablets hinged together, the central one being the largest) and four-panel kinds. For display they required no supporting object to lean against, nor was it necessary to squeeze them by a corner into a picture frame or mirror; they stood on their own on a mantel-piece, piano or table. The triptych usually had short supporting 'legs' like a screen for excluding draughts.

The panels of all types had pictures and verses on the inside, with designs, usually flowers, on the back panels, two of which became the front when closed.

A charming small two-panel card by Marcus Ward & Company has on the left a girl in a white dress with a dove on her hand; she is surrounded by blue flowers. On the right a little Miss in a pale red skirt and white blouse sits deep in thought in a bower of pink flowers. The surrounding decorative borders are in green and gold. The panels on the reverse have white flowers and birds on a deep pink background, gold-framed. The verses may be seen by moving back the pictures, which are secured at the base only.

Some handsome triptych types that were eagerly bought by discriminating shoppers included a large screen (9 × 8 inches when open) by Raphael Tuck & Sons. This winter scene, so ably painted by R. F. McIntyre, shows a huge tree whose branches spread into the adjoining panels. The left panel depicts workmen in the snow watched by an inquisitive dog; on the extreme right is a woodland view, while the centre panel has two men, one sitting down, the other with what appears to be long branches of holly strapped to his back. The sentiment is 'May fairest gifts of earth and heaven to you this Christmas morn be given'. But, being a Scot, the artist worked in a favourite expression: 'For Auld Lang Syne'.

The other side of the screen has forget-me-nots and the Christmas rose (*Helleborus niger*) which was introduced into gardens in England in the sixteenth century and is now a popular

35. *What was said to have been a combined Christmas–Birthday card for those born around Christmas time, is a very attractive panel produced by Marcus Ward. It shows two young girls in two entirely different moods: one happy to sit among the flowers with a dove on her hand, the other with her head bowed down on her arm deep in thought.*

---

plant cultivated here and in the USA for Christmas decorations. A verse by Pope completes this attractive item.

A triptych from De La Rue's Series No. 1 consists of a brilliantly coloured painting of a Brazilian Troupiale, on either side of which are verses by a poet whose name is not shown, but they are so expressive they are worthy of being repeated here. The first represents the thoughts of the bird; the second, 'Content', is the poet's dream – and that of many of us.

FOR AULD

MAY FAIREST GIFTS OF EARTH AND HEAVEN
TO YOU THIS CHRISTMAS MORN BE GIVEN!

LANG SYNE.

36. *A large triptych (9 in × 8 in open) designed as*
a screen by Raphael Tuck. The winter scene spread
over the three panels was painted by R.F. McIntyre.
A Christmas rose and forget-me-nots appear on the
reverse.

CLING TO JESUS.

WORSHIP CHRIST, THE NEW-BORN KING.

GLORY BE TO GOD.

Come, ye Children blithe and merry,
This one Child, your model make,
Christmas holly, leaf and berry,
All be prized, for his dear sake.

E.A.M.   1875.

Brazilian Troupiale

Far in Brazilia's forest-tangled bower,
Where the lush creepers, stirred by no
    faint breeze,
With their green canopy festoon the trees,
And through the moon-lit night each
    new-born hour
Unfolds the bell of its own signal-flower,
I lead a joyous round of lazy ease,
The bright-hued insects in their flight I seize,
And dally with the sun's meridian power;
For me no terrors hath the wintry gloom;
Not often doth the fatal tread of men,
Bent on the winning of my painted plume,
Intrude upon the quiet of my glen;
And when at length death calls me to my tomb,
My life exhales 'midst wastes of wild perfume.

Content

Mine be a cot beside a sheltering hill,
Hard by a wood-side, far from fashion's lure;
Near, let a brawling brook with water pure
Ever make music with its murmured trill;
Mine be enough the cheery cup to fill

37. *W.A. Mansell of London had many beautiful religious cards designed for them, also silhouette types. The triptych here pictures Baby Jesus in the arms of the Virgin Mary. Dated 1875.*

Of welcome guest, or help the wandering poor;
My dog lie by me, my companion sure,
And the tame wild-birds haunt my
    window sill;
A tiny garden-patch surround my door
Where flowers, that load the air with natural
    scent,
Entice my bees; a choice and copious store
Of favourite books; and with these goods
    content,
If God grant health and friends, I ask no more:
Here let my still and even life be spent.

On the back of this card is an unusual feature: a small hinged easel that lifts up to form a support when displaying the card. It has these words:

With dainty finger – lest I break,
And you impute to me the blame –

Lift me, and lo! a stand I make,
A tiny easel to this frame.

The side panels shut to reveal two gates in gold on a brown background and the greeting 'With the Compliments of the Season'.

Another triptych, marked 1880, has as a centrepiece a beautiful spray of pink rhododendrons, with verses on either side. On the back, again in brown and gold, there are little angels above the usual compliments, and on the centre panel a hinged card, with another angel, which can be raised to enable the whole card to stand up.

There were quite a number of religious cards of the three-panel type, an attractive one of which shows Baby Jesus in the arms of His mother. Above this picture are the words 'Worship Christ, The New-Born King'; the panels left and right have 'Cling to Jesus' and 'Glory be to God', each on a cross, all in gold. The outside panels are pale mauve with gold ivy leaves and 'A Christmas Present'. It is dated 1875, and the publisher was W. A. Mansell of Oxford Street.

A large four-panel screen (15 × 6 inches open) by Raphael Tuck & Sons has water lilies on each panel, while on the reverse are brown leaves and branches with large red birds in flight; the background is yellow.

SETS

Many of the big publishers issued sets of cards in which the shape, frame and colours were identical; only the central designs were different, although related to one subject.

Raphael Tuck & Sons were responsible for many fine sets of both the single and the folded types. In the artistic series an attractive card shows in the central countersunk design children on a swing or in a hammock; the frame is in shades of green with small birds in gold, and on the back are verses by Helen Marion Burnside.

A set in small format has brief quotations from the Bible in gold, black and red letters decorated with sprigs of flowers, and in the lower left-hand corner in very small letters 'Mildmay'; this was the name of a series of religious Christmas cards of the 1870s–'80s handled by W. H. Lever of London.

38–40. Sets of cards very briefly illustrating an incident or developing a simple theme make a fascinating page or two in an album. Hildesheimer & Faulkner issued some fine sets, one specimen of which is shown here; it is of small format (2 in × 3¼ in), beautifully coloured, the simple design showing young children draped in many flowers. 1890 is the date given on the back.

A dainty set by Hildesheimer & Faulkner, with the date 1890 on the reverse, has on each card children adorned with flowers. A gold frame encloses the pale grey background.

Alfred Gray of London (1870s) published some amusing cartoons which he also helped to create and colour with a collaborator, cartoonist W. G. Baxter. One set shows two mischievous boys, one planning to trip up a fat policeman by using an umbrella, the other preparing to pelt him with snowballs as soon as he finishes chatting up a servant girl. The captions on the cards appear as 'No. 1. Ye humble plot of ye wicked urchins'; 'No. 2. Ye amazement of ye kind-hearted Peeler', and so on.

Another 'sequence' type briefly telling a story was published by Hildesheimer & Faulkner for Christmas and New Year. Designed in England and printed in Germany, it opens with six schoolboys having a disastrous pillow fight in their dormitory. A following picture shows the elderly headmaster, with a lighted candle and a cane, framed in the doorway

Wishing you a joyous Christmas.

Nº 2 Yᵉ amazement of yᵉ kind-hearted Peeler

surveying this scene of destruction, while the boys hide wherever they can, two of them in a wrecked bed. What the consequence was I know not, for my set of this series is incomplete.

A set from Eyre & Spottiswoode, one card of which is dated 1880, is shaped like a horse-shoe; in the centre appears the large head of a horse, a different breed for each brass-coloured horseshoe.

Marcus Ward issued a set of child studies, head and shoulders, beautifully drawn and coloured in golden yellow, the portraits set off

41–42. Here we have a humorous incident by W.G. Baxter, the cartoonist, based on an idea by Alfred Gray. The 'story' unfolded in the set shows the 'wicked urchins' teasing 'ye kind-hearted Peeler'.

by a grey frame. The greeting is in gold in imitation handwriting. The date on the reverse of one card is 1889.

Aubry Ed. of Paris created a set of small cards in the 1870s called 'Souvenir'. They had a common design of various flowers, but each had a small bunch of flowers, different for each card, hinged over a message, 'Wishing you a Merry Christmas and a Happy New Year', revealed when the flowers were bent back. These French cards are sometimes found in British scrap books, for they were distributed in London and elsewhere by Marion & Company of Soho Square.

The ever-popular cats and dogs, frosted cottages in the snow, babies in bed with their dog or cat sprawling beside them, a neat little gilt-edged set of sailing boats at sea, bouquets and sprays of flowers, an amusing owl set, little girls in Greenaway-style dresses skipping or trying to catch a butterfly, frosted churches and trees in winter scenes – all these attractive subjects and very many more appeared in sets of two, four, six or even twelve cards.

When the folded card appeared in the shops it became more popular than the single type, although the latter came back into favour with the introduction of the 'comics'. Many sets of the folded variety continued the idea of having similar styles and usually the same colours, but with slight variations in design, making for a pleasing continuity.

Raphael Tuck & Sons struck a different note in some of their serrated-edged floral sets in the greetings, such as 'Rich Blessings', 'Much Joy and Favour to You' and 'Health and Fair Greetings'. One of their colourful series had the different greeting on each card placed on three Chinese lanterns on a background of holly and ivy, and irregular-shaped edges with the base folded up a little concealing the sender's name. A similar style continued on a set with designs of country scenes on a palette; also on a horizontal set with the flowers in shades of green.

Another attractive series in vertical format has two imitation clasps or hinges extended out on the left of the card which shows pink flowers on a ribbed green background with 'Good Wishes', 'Best Wishes', 'To Greet You', and so on, in pink and gold on a white base. The wishes inside are also in gold.

Anyone wishing to feature some of these cards in his or her collection might wonder how they can be obtained in complete sets. Searching for them can be a slow task and often one has to be content with two or three examples; but it is sometimes possible to find complete unused sets at fairs or shows where ephemera and second-hand books are on offer.

As with all collecting hobbies, when completion of a particular group or set is desired, the pleasure in searching for elusive items and suddenly finding them is a joy that only a true collector can appreciate.

43. *Horses of all breeds are popular as a theme. A short set by Eyre & Spottiswoode is particularly attractive because it depicts a well-drawn head of a horse in a large horseshoe cut to shape. The specimen shown here is dated 1880.*

FIVE

Novelties and photography

JAPANESE STYLES

A delightful group of cards can be found depicting Westernized drawings of Japanese characters and scenes. But why the sudden appearance of designs from a faraway country in the Far East on Christmas cards bought chiefly by English ladies?

The fashion (or craze) for things Japanese started towards the end of the nineteenth century. Perhaps it was a mild revolt against the austerity of Victorian patriotic feeling or the development of the aesthetic movement. Whatever the reason it was a fact that objects from Japan and imitations of them occupied the leisure moments of some gentlewomen whilst they floated about their boudoirs in brilliantly coloured kimonos, or shaded themselves from the sun with sunshades of oiled silk or paper instead of the normal parasols.

Much favoured, too, were Japanese fans, one of which could be used effectively during a social evening to act as a silent messenger able to convey a discreet invitation across a ballroom.

When the craze spread to certain Christmas cards, many attractive series produced in Britain came on the market. But although there

44. *Towards the end of the nineteenth century many middle-class women took up a new craze — all things Japanese, and card publishers welcomed the novelty. In this painting we see a man holding a fan; he wears a kimono and a skirt and has a small moustache; storks in the stream attract his attention. 1880 is the date of this card printed in exceedingly fine colours.*

45. (below) *A well-dressed Japanese lady and her child haughtily watch a mask-maker painting his creation. The verse on the back tells us she threw the mask away. Like most westernized Japanese cards this specimen is brightly coloured.*

46. (left) *The lady of culture on this card of the 1880s trips sedately past a tree with pink blossoms, while her maid protects her from the sunshine with a huge umbrella.*

47. (right) *Another Japanese specimen that adds interest to this group, for it reminds us that in Imperial days a well-to-do lady wore a dress that swept the ground, whereas her servant wore a shorter dress revealing her shoes. The little lady with a large fan has her 'attendant' to protect her.*

far as Christmas cards were concerned, some British publishers produced a number of designs that captured the popular conception of certain Japanese social activities.

Marcus Ward & Company in 1878–80 issued attractive cards designed by Percy Tarrant (flowers, etc.) and T. Walter Wilson (a Japanese lacquer cabinet). De La Rue & Company commissioned Rebecca Coleman in 1879 to include some Japanese designs in her work for them. One of these was a beautiful study of a girl with a sunshade which occupied the whole area of the card.

An embossed card, with parts of the flowers at the top extended as a cut-out, shows two children, one with a large fan, the other (her 'attendant') with a sunshade protecting her little charge from the sun – or perhaps the rain?

A noble lady graces a small card that appeared in the 1880s. She is shown by a blossoming apple tree accompanied by her maid dutifully shielding her mistress with a tent-like umbrella on which appears 'A Merry Christmas'.

Another small card has a brightly dressed mother and her equally brightly dressed child stopping to look at a man squatting down and painting masks, with other examples of his craft beside him. The child would like one of the masks, but the mother is not impressed by them. The verse on the reverse starts:

> I painted a mask for my lady
> To wear upon Christmas day,
> But my lady she was disdainful
> And threw my mask away.

On another card is a painting of a man carrying a fan and wearing a pink and beige kimono, and a pale blue skirt (the small moustache indicates his masculinity); he is contemplating two storks in a stream. The black background sets off this picture nicely. It is a thick vertical card with a dark brown reverse having a verse by 'P.M.H.' in a frame supported by reeds and flowers (1880).

These Japanese-style single cards are not too easy to come across, so they are well worth a search.

had always been great originality in Japanese art, British publishers were not very original in their choice of subjects to represent the culture of Japan. Was the work of a master such as Hokusai (1790–1849) too original, his views of Mount Fuji on his *surimona* (greeting card prints) too delicate for popular Western Christmas cards?

Japanese paintings reveal an art form that no other country, except perhaps China or Korea, can successfully emulate. However, as

48. (left) *This glamorous little girl of Hildesheimer & Faulkner was drawn in 1884 by 'L.L.', initials that stand for Lizzie Lawson.*

49. (below) *Another circular card, a tambourine, has a little girl holding a round box of what appear to be candies. The publisher was Siegmund Hildesheimer of London, a very important firm in the trade up to 1890.*

50. (right) *Stop thief! That was the cry of all the dogs chasing a dog running off with a chicken, an exciting chase on a palette design, a shape that became very popular. Wolff Hagelberg of Berlin, London and New York were the publishers.*

A merry Christmas.

Stop thief! oh what a hue and cry
See how they chase one hungry sinner!
I almost hope he'll get away,
And eat in peace his Christmas dinner!
But I wish you whate'er may befall
A Merry Christmas one and all

E. E. G.

ODD SHAPES

The single card of rectangular shape was in vogue for many years from 1843. There seems to have been a preference for the small size, not for its cheapness but because people who were getting into the habit of sending such greetings to their friends preferred the simplicity and the neatness of the early format of the visiting card with unobtrusive design, such as flowers or a crest.

In the 1880s and into the early part of the twentieth century cards of all shapes and sizes appeared; some quite artistic, others comical and better suited to the younger generation.

One of the most popular shapes was circular and there are some very attractive designs that can add a touch of youthful glamour to a display, such as a gilt-edged one (Hildesheimer & Faulkner) showing the head and shoulders of a little girl. Near the wording 'Christmas greetings with love' appear the initials 'L.L.' representing Lizzie Lawson (dated 1884). This

artist produced similar studies for a number of other publishers.

Siegmund Hildesheimer & Company of London and New York, who apparently dominated the trade from 1877 to 1890, also produced circular cards of good design, and these should be represented in one's collection. Their name is usually printed in very small type on the left of the base.

Cards of a round shape, although attractive looking, did not remain very popular for long, as they required special square envelopes for posting, but they were the delight of many a Victorian boy and girl on twelfth night when the decorations came down and opposing forces, facing each other on opposite ends of the room, deftly flicked cards at the 'enemy', a direct hit counting as one point. Such missiles flying backwards and forwards at a great speed would bring forth battle cries that in turn would bring an irate parent and an end to a noisy contest. A simple game of many days

gone by, the recounting of which seems to have been lost in the shadows of time.

The palette, with its thumb hole, was another favourite. A quite amusing one shows two little monkeys chasing each other through this thumb hole. It was designed in England by a Hildesheimer & Faulkner artist and printed in Germany. Another palette has a dog running off with a chicken in its mouth, presumably snatched from a dinner table, and being chased by eight more hungry dogs; the verse by 'E.E.G.' (E. E. Griffin) reads:

> Stop thief! Oh what a hue and cry
> See how they chase one hungry sinner!
> I almost hope he'll get away,
> And eat in peace his Christmas dinner!
> But I wish you whate'er may befall
> A Merry Christmas one and all.

This was produced by Wolff Hagelberg of Berlin, with branches in London and New York.

Some cards appeared in a large oval shape with irregular scalloped edges, sometimes in gold, such as a winter scene of a church by a small river, produced by Davidson Brothers of London and printed in Germany. Another oval type worth noting has a pierced outer frame that has a look of ivory. The picture is of a girl in a bonnet and pink frock; she is sitting on a fence with a white dove on her shoulder. The verse is by Helen Marion Burnside:

> Little Child with smiling eyes,
> That look so innocent and wise,
> 'Twas such as those – one Christmasday,
> Who in a lowly manger lay –
> And for the children still we make
> High festival for His dear sake.

51. (far left) *Little Child with smiling eyes was the name given to this little lady sitting on a stile with a dove on her shoulder. Court (Greeting) Cards were the publishers, Helen Marion Burnside was the versifier. She wrote about 6,000 verses for English and American firms.*

52. (left) *This single fan was a Wolff Hagelberg card on which the artist portrayed the young blue-eyed girl in an appealing style. The greeting is lightly embossed.*

53. (below) *A young naked girl lies sleeping on the branch of a flowering tree. The Rev. Frederick Langbridge, a writer for Raphael Tuck in the 1870s–80s, composed the verse on the back of this card.*

May your blessings multiply
Ever as the years roll by.

All Happiness be thine this Christmas.

54. *Triangular shapes lent themselves to some attractive arrangements of flowers.*

55. *'I am bursting to wish you a Merry Christmas' says this old boot, one of numerous comic cards that caused many a laugh towards the end of the nineteenth and the beginning of the twentieth centuries.*

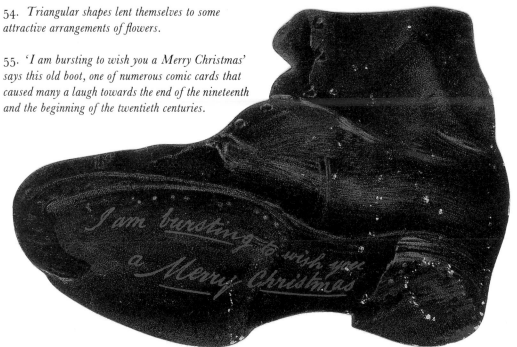

On the back of the card appears 'Court (Greeting) Cards. By Royal Letters Patent. S & N'. From 1870 to the end of that century Miss Burnside was the author of around 6,000 verses for publishers in England and America.

An artistic semi-oval card dated 1884 has a picture of a young naked girl asleep on what appears to be a 'tree' of large honeysuckle. On the back is a sentiment by the Reverend Frederick Langbridge.

Many artistic single fan-shaped cards were issued, and here again Wolff Hagelberg produced some of the most attractive ones printed in Berlin. This firm's artist caught the innocence of a blue-eyed, fair-haired girl. The message 'A bright and happy Christmas' is lightly embossed at the top.

Triangular shapes also added to the variety of greetings, as did crescent-shaped cards. A fine silver edged example of the latter came from Hildesheimer & Faulkner with a design of white flowers and a moon shining on the sea.

In a lighter mood there are the comic cut-outs such as an old top hat with a message on the crown in white 'May you spend a jolly time under the old roof'; also an old dark brown boot with the wording on the sole 'I am bursting to wish you a Merry Christmas'.

A shaped card reveals a 'comfort' Victorians often carried when travelling, particularly in winter, namely a large coloured rug rolled up and secured by straps and a wide handle; there is also a strap stretched between the handles for carrying a newspaper or book. The design appears on both sides and the handles open to reveal a picture of two boats in the distance and cottages by a stream. The words within say 'Unbroken joys be thine today – Thro' every passing hour!' The thought is that this was a Christmas holiday card.

There is one particular type that is becoming a little difficult to find these days due to some enthusiastic stamp collectors acquiring them to add light relief to their collections when displaying stamps at society meetings: the shaped red letter box. There are two specimens worth looking out for. One says 'NOTICE. Next collection Xmas Morning Before Sunrise

56. *Some postal historians like to get hold of these novelties for their philatelic ephemera collections. This specimen opens up to show kittens inside the box examining the letters as they tumble through the slot.*

57. *No one could get cross with this appealing kitten for getting its sum wrong. An attractive cut-out shape.*

6 o'clock 8 o'clock 12 o'clock.' When the door is opened it reveals four kittens watching the letters tumbling through the slot and reading the addresses, one of which has 'Father Xmas with Loving Greetings'. The initials of the artist, 'A.F.L.' appear on one of the envelopes. The appropriate verse on the back of the card is headed 'A Merry Christmas of the good old stamp'.

> May Christmas bring a heavy post
> Of good things to your door,
> When friends, a playful merry host,
> Like these young kittens four;
> Light-hearted as these kittens, too,
> The happy moments run;
> And like this pillar box, may you
> Be bright and full of fun.

The second pillar box has in the times of collection plate 'To greet your Xmas' with a tag under the crown and 'ER VII' which can be moved so that a happy boy suddenly appears on the left or an equally happy dog on the right. This pillar box has a support on the back to enable it to stand on its own.

There are other shapes (or cut outs) that could be mentioned, but let us conclude with an appealing one: a brown kitten resting its paws on a large school slate which has the message 'A Happy Christmas and a bright New Year to you', also an incomplete 'noughts and crosses' and a sum that has been added up incorrectly!

COMPLIMENTS OF THE TRADESMEN

A type of card that has been somewhat neglected by collectors is the one with an advertisement on the back. These were sent out by many tradesmen to their customers, and to inform newcomers to the area where their shops were situated and what merchandise they sold. The neat little cards probably went into the kitchen, rather than on to the drawing-room mantelpiece, and ended up in the kitchen dresser.

Some of the announcements make interesting reading, such as that of P. L. Kingsbury of Fulham Road, London, who offered Christmas and New Year cards at the South Kensington Bazaar: six Christmas cards, assorted, for 1d – 'The cheapest ever known. Owing to the enormous quantity sold last year, great purchases have been made, in order to meet the increased demand this season.' Reference was then made to the small card, with flowers in full colour, on which the advertisement appears: 'This style ... 2¾d per doz ... thousands of DOLLS from 1d to 40s each. Beautiful Models. Immense stock of COLOURED SCRAPS, &c., very cheap, for making Albums, Screens, &c.'

A folded card, visiting card size, depicts an old woman carrying six huge reels of Ferguslie Crochet Cotton; a small white dog makes her task more difficult by jumping up in front of her. The back of the card has a calendar for 1876.

Another shows three small boys, one of whom stands on a table wielding an immense pair of scissors and cutting a large length of blue material held by the others. Above them is a large sign, 'Cut to the latest fashion by the most EXPERIENCED workmen'. This amusing drawing was the trade card of Mawer and Collingham, Drapers, of High Street, Lincoln, and it had a calendar for 1882 on the back.

A robin perched on a large plant singing a song to his mate below and the greeting 'Wishing you a Happy Christmas' is Fisher & Company's card from Norwich, extolling the universally known Diamond Baking and Egg Powders, Denmark Custard Powder and Blancmange Pudding Powder. Another card from this firm depicts three storks riding penny-farthing bicycles and carrying babies with them, and on the base: 'A Delightful Christmas to You'. This firm had a liking for pictures of birds, for on a New Year card three of them are perched on a branch with ivy above and a church in the background.

Henry Milward & Sons, manufacturers of needles, sent to their customers a folded calendar card for 1881. Lithographed by Willott & Grover, it shows on one half of the card a little angel handing over a wall a large packet of needles to two girls, and on the other half a

sailor boy in a rowing boat passing up another large packet of needles to a girl. It is a nicely designed card in brilliant colours.

Peek, Frean & Company of London sent a neat calendar for 1888 to their customers as a reminder at Christmas and the New Year that they baked 250 varieties of biscuits packed in brilliant enamelled boxes – the latter being collectors' pieces today! The two designs on the front of the calendar show birds in delightful settings.

Perhaps one of the most unusual forms of advertising from a trader was thought up by S. Lucking, Grocer, who sent to his special customers attractive flower Christmas cards with handwritten offers on the back, such as:

Christmas 1884

6 Cocker Nuts   1/-
40 Oranges   1/-
8 lbs beautiful Sugar   1/-
Best Spanish Nuts   3d pnt
Chestnuts   3d quart
¼lb beautiful Tea   6d
The celebrated 2/- Tea,
    grand for Christmas

In 1879 there was an Agricultural Exhibition in London. To draw attention to an 'Improved Magic Lantern, showing a Brilliant Lighted Picture 10 or 12 feet in diameter; Endless Amusement for Christmas and Long Winter Evenings', The Sciopticon Company of Great Portland Street, London, advertised their apparatus on the back of a small Christmas card showing a little girl crying because she has dropped a large jug of milk, and a little boy trying to comfort her. The card was given to visitors to the exhibition and also sent to special customers.

A. Pinnick, shirt manufacturers and outfitters of Stratford, issued a small card in colour showing a young lad in a nice clean shirt adjusting his bow tie in front of a mirror, while a young girl attired in a mauve frock stands in the doorway, presumably suggesting that unless the boy hurries they will be late for the party.

R. S. Aitken, draper, milliner and outfitter of Chesham, sent out a pretty calendar card in

1882 showing a couple in a rowing boat, and a verse:

> The Christmas bright as flowers be,
> The New Year bring prosperity

enclosed in a rustic frame.

Henry H. Goddard of Finsbury Park, London, also in 1882, addressed shoppers on a card of red and yellow roses with the comforting words 'Happy Christmas may this be/And many of them may you see.' Apart from that sentiment, his commercial message was 'I am now showing a very large and choice selection of Christmas and New Year Cards at the lowest prices ever offered, and a large variety of Toys, Dolls, Albums and Fancy Articles suitable for Presents.'

It can be a small problem knowing how to display these advertising cards in an album. One method is to use plastic leaves so that both sides of the cards can be seen, or insert them in clear, acid free envelopes, slightly bigger than the card, and secure them by means of a mount at the top and bottom left corners to a white album page so it can be turned back to show the other side. But the neatest way is to take a clear photocopy of the advertisement and mount this either beside the card on the right, or below it.

Although these small advertising cards are not very imposing, they are mentioned here because they form part of our story.

DÉCOUPAGE

Among the unusual and quite attractive Christmas postcards are those whose designs are made up by hand from parts of cut up postage stamps. And in case any puristic philatelists hold up their tweezers in horror at the thought of Penny Blacks being mutilated, let it be stated right away that the specimens used in this strange form of art must always be common stamps in plentiful supply. For the do-it-yourself enthusiasts who have a desire to create a few of their own greeting cards, current British, American and issues of other countries easily available are most suitable for such collages.

The idea is not new, for in our collection are a number of items professionally created by hand by a foreign firm many years ago. On the reverse of the cards appears POST CARD and the trade name of the series: 'Stampcards'. On the specimen illustrated the little girl, the candlelit tree, its stand and table are created out of, mostly, German stamps.

A firm in China also issued these cards, using Japanese stamps, with embellishments by an artist to create very pleasing designs.

These figures cut from postage stamps were also produced by a once famous firm, Alpha Publishing Company Ltd of Scrutton Street, London. In 1913 they issued 24 different designs; they are not easy to find these days.

The Americans appear to have created a new interest in découpage. (The name for this form of design, created by cutting up scraps of small printed paper objects to form pictures, has apparently been accepted, at least in the USA, as découpage, French for cutting up or cutting out.) Many such cards of intricate design have been produced in America, but only those with a Christmas theme concern us here. A few specimens are certainly not amiss in the novelty section of a collection.

A RECORD BREAKER

A very unusual greeting arrived at my home at Christmas time many years ago. It was circular, 4 inches across, with a hole right through it – and the card talked. It was in fact a tiny gramophone record, on the front of which appeared the words 'A MERRY CHRISTMAS AND A HAPPY NEW YEAR'.

Played on a gramophone (78 r.p.m. speed), it revealed itself to be a long personal message from the BBC's first popular radio disc jockey and record critic, the late Christopher Stone. Copies of this record were sent to friends and selected newspaper contacts of this man, at one time the most famous and distinguished presenter of records on radio.

The little record, manufactured by Darium Products G.B. Ltd of Slough, England, was sent from Wiston Old Rectory, Steyning,

58. *This is a Christmas card made from common stamps cut to a shape to form a design, then pasted on a card. These novelties were created many years ago by a few firms in China and also London. Quite a number of American enthusiasts have created some excellent designs and they have called this pastime découpage.*

Sussex. It has a personally signed greeting on the back, with an illustration of a little girl playing the piano with Christmas trees on either side. Today this unusual greeting is a collector's piece.

MUSIC COVERS

One of the joys of searching for Christmas cards in shops and on dealers' stands at hobby fairs is that you never know what unusual item is going to come your way. And of course it always makes it more exciting if you have the instincts of a human magpie with an interest in ephemera.

Searching through a dusty pile of music in a second-hand bookshop in Charing Cross Road one day in search of a Billy Mayerl piano piece (which eventually turned out to be too difficult for my fumbling fingers), I uncovered six sheets of Victorian Christmas dance music that just had to be acquired. The cover of one, 'The Winter Quadrille' by C. H. R. Marriott, was a large drawing in colour of a Christmas card showing a windmill and a girl crossing a snow-covered footbridge over a wide stream, all enclosed in a garland of holly berries, and heavily frosted.

But the real gem was 'A Happy New Year Polka' with 'A Merry Christmas Polka', published by Alphonse Bertini and Company, London. Pasted within a frame on the cover was a small Christmas card of the 1870s showing a small child in a pink costume surrounded by blue forget-me-nots and on the following page a drawing of a holly card with 'A Merry Christmas to You'. Alphonse must have had a good supply of cards, for on the cover of another edition of just the one polka appears a large framed border of holly with the words 'Bertini's Musical Xmas Cards', and pasted on the centrepiece is a beautifully designed card showing a boy and a girl in eighteenth-century costumes carrying a large casket with the greeting 'A Happy Christmas'. The colours are brilliant, as if the card had been recently printed.

The next item was a long pianoforte piece, 'A Christmas Souvenir' by J. Pridham, published by Brewer & Company. Pasted on the cover was a card showing an angel pointing out to two children a picture of the three wise men, with the message below 'A Merry Christmas'. But the outstanding feature was the large separate paper-lace frame of gold and white with small imitation flowers and fern pasted on.

Probably very few of these sheets of music have survived the passing of over a hundred years. Whether out of appreciation of those enterprising music publishers, the novelty of Christmas cards adorning the covers, or perhaps the love of Victoriana, if any collector should be fortunate enough to come across similar relics of a bygone age, he or she would

59. *This photograph is over a hundred years old. It is one of many taken by William Luks from 1880 onwards. Most of them were hand-coloured and the prints then pasted on thick black card with gold edges.*

60. *This child study was from a photograph taken by Robert Faulkner. It was issued as a Christmas card by Hildesheimer & Faulkner.*

61. *A very early photograph of a private dwelling, mounted on a thick card with an ornate frame in black and gold.*

be wise to acquire them; not to be put away in a drawer and perhaps forgotten, but to be framed and hung on a wall, where they would certainly become a talking point!

PHOTOGRAPHY

The interest in early pictures among photographers has never been as prevalent as it is today. With active societies, magazines and exhibitions devoted to the subject, there is no lack of stimulating activity for the countless millions of amateur and professional photographers.

Since the craft was making giant strides in its development during the 1870s, Christmas cards began to appear with pictures created by users of the pioneer cameras and the improved developing processes. As quite an assortment of studies appear on early cards, a most interesting display can be built up to show the artistic ability of the early photographers.

In 1880 William Luks of Bedford Street, Strand, produced many photographic cards. He had them hand-coloured and mounted on thick black card, $4\frac{1}{2} \times 6\frac{3}{4}$ inches in size, with gold edges and a greeting such as 'Wishing you

a Merry Christmas and a Happy New Year' also in gold, and at the base of the card in very small type 'William Luks – Copyright – London'.

His photographs were mostly of outdoor scenes in which trees, tree-lined paths, foliage and streams predominated. A little girl, believed to be his daughter, usually wearing a pink dress, was often used as a model, and there is one delightful scene in which she is gently chasing a squirrel up a tree. While some of the outdoor work is not very brilliant, particularly in an inability to capture the reflection of a stream, his 1884 indoor portraits of children are fine studies.

Luks' coloured photographic cards were usually expertly tinted by hand, for the time had not yet arrived when coloured film made hand-tinting an unnecessary task. The results of many experiments with direct colour photography were too crude to be used commercially, but in 1907 the Lumière Autochrome process, in which carbon black filled the space between the dyed starch grains of the filter layer, resulted in a plate that produced excellent colour work with good commercial possibilities.

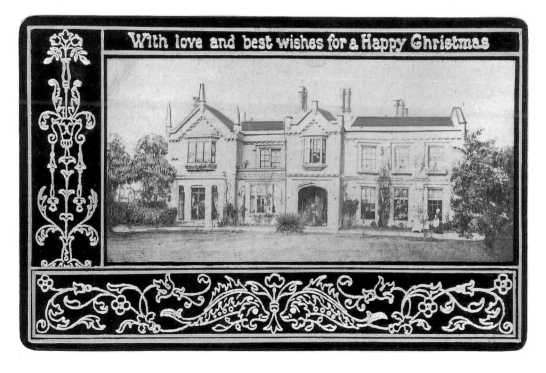

62. *Victorian cards showing small photographic scenes in a vignette as part of the design became popular for a while. This one shows Edinburgh Old Town and Waverley Bridge.*

If the collector intends to go into the twentieth century to add to the collection of photographic cards the prospects are interesting, particularly where the Royal Family is concerned. When Edward VII became King in

1901 Christmas cards of His Majesty and Queen Alexandra were issued with the greeting 'To wish you every happiness under the Old Flag and the New Reign.'

If we venture as far as the dramatic period of 1939–44 (to go farther than this is to get involved in countless modern photographic cards) an outstanding assortment of historical pictures will come into view, but these will be described briefly in the section on World Wars I and II.

HOLD-TO-LIGHT

These HTLs, as collectors sometimes call them, were novelties of 1897–98 that immediately became popular. It was a new idea, attractive and appealing to all children.

They were well produced in a variety of designs and artistic shapes. A number of famous buildings were used in the designs – providing they had plenty of windows; the reason for this was that when the cards were held up to a light the buildings came alive with glowing windows.

During manufacture, the card showing a building with many windows (the Tower of London, for example) had these windows cut out and over the vacant space thin red paper was pasted at the back. For small white lights, perforations were made in the card and the space above the building was also cut out and thin white or pale grey paper pasted over the space. On holding the card up to a light, the windows lit up and the Tower was silhouetted against the sky.

Windsor Castle was similarly treated, and there were other delightful pictures to see of star-studded skies with a moon and perhaps churches whose stained-glass windows shone with coloured lights.

A number of these cards were spoilt by being stuck down in albums. Today's collectors who acquire these novelties are careful to preserve them by slipping them into a single sheet that has a clear protective covering, so the card is easy to remove for the peep-show.

1. *The World's first Christmas envelope. Designed by Richard Doyle and published in December 1840 by (to quote from the base line) 'Messrs. Fores, at their Sporting & Fine Print Repository & Frame Manufactory, 47 Piccadilly – corner of Sackville Strt.'*

2. *The World's first Christmas card. Designed by John Calcott Horsley, RA, from an idea supplied by Henry Cole, 1843. Lithographed by Jobbins of Holborn. Sold at Felix Summerly's Home Treasury Office in Bond Street at one shilling each, but now probably the rarest Christmas card in existence.*

3. The front cover of this card shows a cornucopia of forget-me-nots and underneath this 'May Christmas bring you Happiness'. When the cover is pulled down the picturesque scene that unfolds is a flower-lover's paradise.

4. A 'platform' with the words 'With best Wishes' on the front of this specimen is moved down to complete the picture of a handsome boy and a pretty girl smiling at the receiver of this card. The 'platform' makes this picture self-supporting.

5. These ornate single cards framed by wide coloured silk fringes were among some of the most highly priced greetings available at the time. The two birds are perched on the branches of a rose tree.

A joyful CHRISTMAS.

6. *These beautiful fan cards close together and fold flat just like a real fan. The example shown has flowers and a short sentiment on each segment, and a frilled tassel to hold the fan together.*

7. *Another example of an elegant folding fan, with good wishes for Christmas and the New Year spread over each section.*

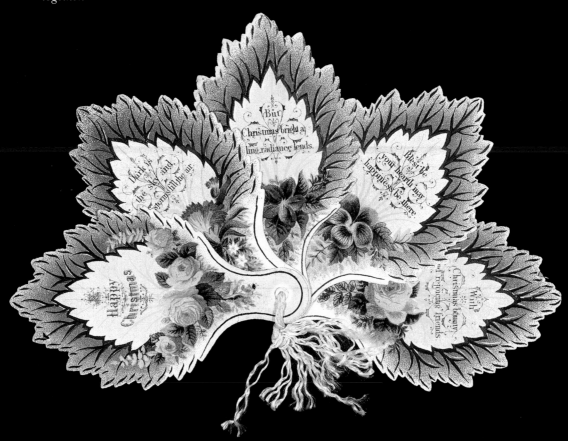

8. A gentle pull on a ribbon and the guardian angels move forward from the clouds to watch the sleeping child. The wings of the angels shimmer from the frosting on them.

9. *When the forget-me-nots of the lyre are pulled forward this piece can stand on its own and it then reveals pink paper roses that open up. These 'action' cards were treasured so much that for over a hundred years they have been carefully looked after by succeeding owners so that many are still in good condition today.*

10. *'Ye Christmas Pantomime' takes place at the Theatre and the well-dressed theatre-goers move through the doors in dignified excitement. The stage comes into view when side panels are pulled back and we see the players in action.*

11. *An oval of flowers moves down by operating a tab, revealing a seasonal message and a picture in an uncovered window. Like most of the cards of this type the frames are well adorned and gold plays an important part.*

12. *A children's party in full swing is the happy scene that comes to life when the exterior of a large house is opened. When the side panels are moved back the drawing-room is extended, giving the youngsters ample room for their noisy festivity and merriment.*

13. *More flowers conceal the secret messages behind them, easily revealed when a chord is pulled: the flowers droop and the messages can be read.*

14. *A pull on another tab card shows four happy scenes, each in its own oval: a man at a dinner party proposing a toast, a young girl sewing, a young man offering gifts to a young lady and a girl helping another with her wedding veil. An obvious little story here.*

63. 'Hold To Light' cards became one of the most popular of the novelties, irrespective of the ages of the recipients. All the windows of the Tower of London in this view glow when the card is held up to a light.

SIX

Humour and hard times

In the early days of Christmas cards, humour, when featured, was in a light vein usually involving the antics of animals and children. But as the novelty of snow scenes, holly and robins became commonplace, artists were encouraged to use more originality in their work to keep up the interest of customers of a rapidly growing seasonal market.

So it was that more designs of a humorous nature began to appear in the shops, and the pranks of children, and of animals dressed as humans, joined the contrived 'humour' of unfortunate men falling through the ice, clowns knocking down policemen and other such happenings that often raise unsympathetic laughter from the onlooker but never the victim. The captions are usually quite amusing, but were probably more so at the time they first appeared, especially if they were topical.

A delightful series called 'Christmas Advances', dated 1879, by Marcus Ward Ltd, shows on one card a young lady in a beautiful dress disdainfully rejecting a humanized Christmas pudding on its knees, clutching the hem of her dress and obviously asking a special favour, such as to be eaten by her. The verse cautions her thus:

> Fair Girl be warned
> When Christmas comes
> Reject that pudding
> Stuffed with plums.

Cards by John A. Lowell & Company of Boston, USA, sometimes appear in albums made up by Victorian children and adults over 100 years ago. This does not necessarily indi-cate that the cards were sent to them by friends or relatives in America, for the Boston company had an agent, Lawrence Brothers, who acted for them in London in the 1880s.

Many of Lowell's products were steel engraved. One set had a small design partly overlapping a larger one framed by some foliage. The imprint varied from 'Copyrighted by John A. Lowell & Co, Boston, 1897' to 'J. A. Lowell & Co, Boston. Pat. applied for'.

Another attractive short set is shaped like a circular fan and depicts an anxious man leaping over a fence, with an angry bull close on his heels.

A. Ackermann (London 1880s) issued a card by E. A. S. Douglas who brought out the humour of a hunting scene in which an elderly would-be hunter clutches his horse's neck for dear life, as the animal suddenly refuses to take a low hedge. My lady Diana, sitting demurely side-saddle on a white beast, calls to the frightened man, 'Send him at it Uncle and you're bound to go over.' (Ackermann was the British agent for Louis Prang of the USA.)

Little Victorian maidens were not all sugar and spice and all things nice. An 1870s card shows a well-dressed girl holding up her dog to terrify a cat on a windowsill.

One large card published by Marcus Ward & Company in 1873 shows two farmers standing in a sty contemplating four pigs. Says one of the men, 'They're doomed for Christmas, brawn and chine, for pigs must die that men may dine.' The heading to this not very comical scene is 'The compliments of the season, and all good things in reason.' The artist was Henry Stacy Marks, a celebrated member of

64. *The musicians of this frog band play against cut-out windows heavy with thick icicles. Siegmund Hildesheimer & Co issued this amusing card.*

65. *A man about to sit down and having the chair suddenly pulled from under him is supposed to be funny – so thought the clown on this card. The caption above 'May Fortune Be Never Chairy of Her Favour' was added to the picture by Samuel K. Cowan who, in 1884 wrote over a thousand verses for a number of firms.*

66. *An upturned cart and a singing robin are the only comforts available to this man caught in a snow storm. Another example of Victorian humour in adversity.*

MAY YOU SPEND A MERRY CHRISTMASTIME.

A Jolly Christmas to you, old fellow.
People call you "Grand Old Man,"
Treat you like some wondrous god;
But when folks ask your "Home Rule plan,"
Your only answer is a "Nod".

67. *'May you spend a merry Christmastime' is the sarcastic wish to this man unable to sleep because of the cats' wassailing noise.*

68. *The Grand Old Man Gladstone appears on this card which, with the aid of a concealed tiny weight behind, moves his head in either direction '. . . when folks ask your "Home Rule plan" your only answer is a nod.' A scarce political item.*

the Royal Academy who acted as one of the judges at the Dudley Gallery in London when Raphael Tuck held an exhibition in 1880 to select the best designs for prospective cards.

A four-piece frog band playing in the snow was one of the amusing designs of Siegmund Hildesheimer & Company. The icicles hanging from the four cut-out spaces behind the 'musicians' are quite heavy with applied frosting, even after so many years.

It is a delight to form a collection of Louis Wain cats. They were brilliantly drawn; their antics very amusing when imitating human activities. They were seldom overdressed, for the artist relied on expressions and mischievousness to bring out the feline humour. Although a lot of his work appeared on post-

cards during the 1900s, quite a few Wain Christmas cards exist, but they take some finding today.

The lampooning of the aesthetic craze that appeared on cards from 1880–90 caused much amusement. The cards are usually of the flat (single) type. Designs to look for include those by Alan Ludovici Jr, such as the one showing a young man standing in a drawing room and holding at arm's length a large flower at which he gazes ecstatically, while holding his head in painful pleasure. In another picture the same person is sprawled on a chair, elbow resting on a table, and staring with rapt attention at a vase of flowers; the inevitable open fan is on the wall above him.

The same artist portrayed a bonneted lady wearing a long pink dress, standing by a screen and holding before her a large brown teapot which, judging by her loving expression, obviously means the world to her. In the pale green daffodil border are the words 'May you have

69. *The 'Aesthetic Movement'. Here is society at its silliest. The lady has fallen in love with a tea pot and wanders round the drawing room talking to it. This portrayal was by Alan Ludovici, Jr, and Hildesheimer & Faulkner published it.*

70. *This monochrome picture could disillusion young children about Santa Claus: he wears a short fur-trimmed jacket, black tights with white stockings and pointed shoes. He looks mournfully at his message 'A most Consummate XMAS & an utterly utter New Year.' The little aesthetic girl holds a long stemmed flower and on her sash is the date 1882.*

a quite too happy time'. Hildesheimer & Faulkner produced these cards.

There are other amusing designs, certainly worth a search, with affected characters silently raving over flowers, fans or peacock feathers, with titles such as 'Distinctly ineffable,

Oh Son of Apelles', 'The effeminate Aesthetic subject', 'Simpering simplicity' and 'Insufferably too exquisitely dreadful'.

A smaller card in monochrome with a gold border depicts a precious, mournful-looking Santa Claus wearing a short white fur-trimmed jacket and black tights. A little girl stands beside him in a long frock with the date 1881 on the sash, and in her hand a long-stemmed flower. She stares ahead with wide eyes, and is probably Santa's aesthetic daughter.

It is believed that the 'Aesthetic Movement', as practised by the middle classes with nothing better to do, faded out at about the time the so-called 'Naughty '90s' emerged – the latter term fortunately applicable to but a small section of carefree society. Unlike the previous 'Movement', there are no Christmas cards to reflect their activities – which is probably just as well.

To conclude this excursion into the comical aesthetic movement, mention should be made of a postcard-size card showing a member of the aesthetic society, wearing a long blue dress with large puff sleeves, holding a sunflower in one hand and in the other a large peacock fan (both symbols of the 'Movement'); she gazes at nothing in particular, since she is in a self-induced trance. The card is faintly inscribed in the pattern of the blue carpet 'F.A.B. 1881', and on the back is the verse by Ada:

> I have an aim, a noble aim
> (Not very fixed or clear)
> And I must great reform proclaim,
> In this, and many a year.
> Ideas, emotions, grand, intense,
> Which shallow minds have not;
> Results of some 'experience',
> (I do not quite know what).
> I have passed, in meditation,
> Through many a 'mood' and 'phase';
> Till I join in adoration
> Of this aesthetic craze!

71. *One more member of the 'Movement'. An expensively dressed lady holds a large sunflower and a peacock fan. She is in an obvious trance. Apart from gently ridiculing the 'craze' the artist has created a delightful picture of a fashion, a handsome girl and an artistic background.*

THE PUN CARDS

When Angus Thomas came to the City of London in 1883 it was to publish comic Christmas and puzzle cards. The business was successful because a large section of the public took to this new style of single card with silly puns.

For a while the firm monopolized the trade in this type of comic card. Their style was aimed at people seeking a change from traditional greetings to something of a comical nature. The humour was almost childlike: contrived and based on simple puns, but appealing to the majority of younger people wanting to send a silly type of greeting to someone 'for a giggle'.

These joke cards were nearly all of the single type and although they were considered rather lowbrow they became popular. Their sales lasted into the twentieth century.

Examples of the Angus Thomas cards include a patriotic one issued during the Boer War. It shows the Union Jack, the Royal Standard, an actual piece of string tied with a knot to form a noose and the wording: 'The Latest Noose From The Transvaal! "Thro' trying to STEYN Our Flag KRUGER'S GONE OFF HIS TWIST" and feels VERY MUCH HUNG UP Because BULLER'S GOT HIM "ON A LITTLE BIT OF STRING ... Now We CAN enjoy ourselves this CHRISTMAS, and I hope YOU will have A VERY JOLLY TIME with nothing whatever TO BOER YOU."'

A favourite in my collection is a card with a pasteboard thermometer attached at the top by a tiny loop. The message is: 'With Warmest Christmas Greetings. May Your Enjoyment Rise by Degrees to the Highest Known Tem-

72. *Peace for Christmas is the message on this pun card that makes fun of the Boer War leader. The piece of string is real, likewise the wording on the card for those suffering through the war in South Africa. An early and scarce Angus Thomas card.*

73. *A delightful comic card in the Angus Thomas style, with a 'mobile piece' to demonstrate the warmest greetings.*

perature. P.S. What is the Highest Known Temperature? (For answer, see under Thermometer.)' When the little thermometer is lifted up it reveals the answer: '2 (TWO) in the Shade'.

H. H. & CO's UNIQUE SERIES was the imprint on some cards of 1887–90, one of which has stuck on the card a rail ticket dated 25.12.89 with the wording 'FROM CHRISTMAS 1889 my wish to thee and all of thine is best of all wishes "HEALTH DIVINE"' and on the return half of the ticket 'TO THE WORLD'S END for what's the use of riches, honour, wealth if with all these you cannot have "Good Health"'. The main wording on the card is 'Just The Ticket To Wish You a 1st Class Time. Simply this and nothing more!'

It would be unfair to ridicule these pun cards, for they usually caused some amusement to those who received them. Don't we often hear this type of play on words on radio and television today by certain comedians? It would appear that our sense of simple humour has not changed much since the late Victorian days.

HARD TIMES

Students of social and industrial history know the times over the last 150 years when poverty became so apparent that many people of means realized it was about time something was done about the problem. Great reformers such as Charles Dickens, Lord Shaftesbury and Dr Barnardo, to name but a few of the caring Victorians, lashed out with voice and pen against the neglect of the poor.

Christmas cards being a gentle reflection of changes in social life – habits, dress, inventions, pastimes – the degrees of poverty that affected certain classes did not escape the attention of card manufacturers. In the 1880s and '90s 'Hard Times' cards began to appear, usually looking austere, made up of inferior pasteboard, string for ribbon, and with short verses, often quite humorous, reflecting the sender's apparent lack of money.

But it must be admitted that these economy products did not set out to improve the lot of the poor, and in any case it would be difficult to see how they could do that; rather were they an inexpensive novelty that raised a smile and not a tear. However, those who were able to afford more ornate greetings might have had second thoughts on whether to buy expensive cards or not during difficult times, and hopefully the money saved might have been used for a slightly increased cash gift when tradesmen came round for their 'Christmas Box'.

To digress for a moment, there are a few churches today that, during the festive celebrations, place in the vestibule a very large folded card with a seasonal drawing on the front, hand coloured and the work of someone with artistic abilities. Next to the card on a table is a box and a notice to the effect that parishioners who normally send each other cards might like to forego this ritual and place in the box a percentage of the money usually spent on cards and postage. They then sign their name on the large card, happy in the knowledge that the money given is eventually distributed to those in need. I don't think the greeting card publishers are worried about this minute loss of revenue.

An amusing austerity card of 1903 was a luggage label of poor quality pasteboard with a piece of red ribbon tied through the hole where normally a piece of string would go. At the top of the label the name of the senders 'Mr. & Mrs. Geo. Hd. Gay' is printed, and on the back:

> Times are hard, yes, very hard,
> And really we are not able,
> To send our Greeting otherwise,
> But on this luggage label.

A halfpenny green Edwardian stamp, postmarked SCARBOROUGH, carried the label on its very short journey. The local office in 1892 was 46 Queen Street, Scarborough.

A 'court' card ($4\frac{1}{2} \times 3\frac{1}{2}$ inches) by a London publisher was headed 'My Christmas Greeting. The Only Brown' and shows an embossed bronze one penny coin, below which is a verse:

> The times are bad, I'm in an awful fix,
> Commenced the day with just – 2/6.

To live I hied at small expense,
But Dinner landed me for – 18d.
To have no tea! – who would be willing?
So, Nolens volens, I changed the – 1/-.
And now here's Xmas: my wants are many,
But all I have is a single – 1d.

[*Nolens volens* – whether willing or not.]

A larger card in deep red and gold has the verse:

I fear to send this card to you,
Lest haply you may draw
Conclusion from the sending
That I only care
[here a straw was stapled horizontally across the card]
'Tis not so, I assure you!
The fact is 'Times are bad'.
And I only could procure you
The best for what I had.
Wishing you A MERRY XMAS & A HAPPY
NEW YEAR.

A folded card with the greeting on the front in imitation Old English type was tied by a thin green ribbon secured by a large red seal front and back, with a drawing inside of early English carol singers performing outside a large building; underneath this:

No doubt you will have often heard
That 'times are very hard',
But, spite of threatened poverty,
I've bought this little Card;
Like widow's mite, to show you that
My love has never ceas'd,
And make you have a thought for me,
Through Christmas' merry feast.

Postcards raising the question of financial problems appeared very early in the twentieth century. One example worth noting was issued by Birn Brothers in 1903. This firm opened up as stationers in 1882 in London. Their post-cards of high quality were printed in Saxony. One fine specimen has a drawing of a label with robins and holly lightly embossed in colour and underneath this a verse:

I sincerely regret I'm unable
These hard times a present to send;
I can only just manage the label:
Take the will for the deed, old Friend.

This firm's cards are worth looking out for; sometimes the full name is not shown, but their products may still be recognized by the small initials 'B.B.' and 'London'.

74. *Many of these stamp cards had real specimens stuck on them – but not for long when there were young collectors in the family.*

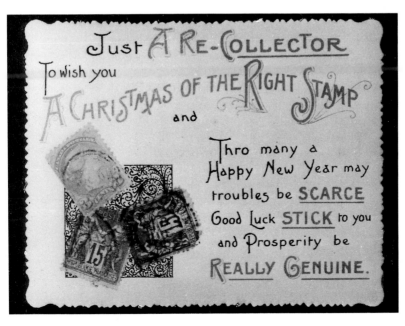

Just A Re-Collector
To wish you
A Christmas of the Right Stamp
and
Thro many a Happy New Year may
troubles be SCARCE
Good Luck STICK to you
and Prosperity be
REALLY GENUINE.

SEVEN

Post Office greetings and the Savings Bank

It is appropriate that the General Post Office should have fostered the habit of exchanging Christmas cards among its heads of departments at the festive season; appropriate because after all the British Post Office, through its numerous departments, makes it possible for people everywhere to send and receive greetings in their many, many millions each year.

One of the items which collectors today like to add to their albums is known as a Post Office Inter-Departmental Christmas card. This sort of card is quite elusive, but again it may be mentioned that it is always worthwhile attending an ephemera fair or a national stamp exhibition and ask the dealers if they have any such items available. But one should 'shop around' before paying a high price. (What is a high price? It could be two or even three figures.)

The details here are based on specimens in my collection, the first of which is dated 1879–80. The design shows the national emblems in a shield surmounted by a crown. Underneath the shield is the wording 'The Officers of the Foreign Department General Post Office London to their colleagues at' and below is a line for the recipient's name; then comes 'A Merry Christmas and a Happy New Year'. The whole design is enclosed in a wide frame of holly leaves, and the colour is brown on white.

A second edition appeared with lettering and surrounds in gold, and with the printer's name under the frame on the right: 'Maclure & Macdonald. Photo-lith'.

The following year came a card bearing a drawing of the General Post Office, London, in a wide circle. On the left is the date 1880 and on the right 1881. 'Christmas & New Year' is above, while below is 'With Fraternal Greetings' in a panel over a large VR and the Royal arms, all in gold on a pale blue-green background.

The next card shows another view of London, this time a section of the Thames Embankment, a bridge, Cleopatra's Needle, a postman, a girl posting a letter in a pillar box, and in the distance St Paul's Cathedral, all in a circle. In the top left and right corners appear 1881 and 1882 respectively. The greeting is 'The Officers of the General Post Office London send greetings and best wishes to their colleagues at' with a space below for a name. The colours are brown, red-brown and gold.

A similar greeting to the one above appears on the card for 1882–3 and the design is appropriate to the season: a field in winter time on the left and a view of St Paul's across the river on the right. Both drawings are in a circle and below is a country scene of snow and a postman emptying a letter box. The usual holly and ivy link up the vignettes, and the printing is black on white.

The card for 1883–4 is one that many collectors of postal history seek but don't often find. This is a facsimile of the Mulready envelope. The standard greeting from the G.P.O. officers is in the centre and below in the margin (referring to the envelope): 'First used on the introduction of the penny postage 1839.' Holly, mistletoe and a large VR appear in the wide margins, and the colours are green and pale green on white.

As to the statement that the Mulready was first used in 1839, this is open to question, for

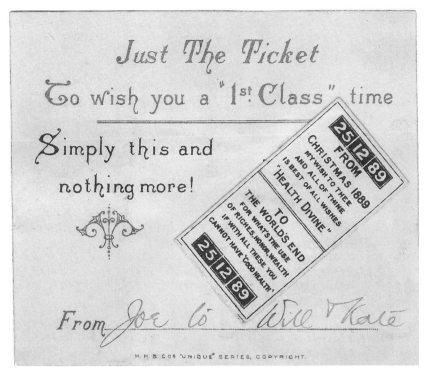

Just The Ticket
To wish you a "1st Class" time
Simply this and
nothing more!

From Joe to Will & Kate

25|12|89 FROM CHRISTMAS 1889 MY WISH TO THEE AND ALL OF THINE IS BEST OF ALL WISHES "HEALTH DIVINE" TO THE WORLD'S END FOR WHAT'S THE USE OF RICHES, HONOR, WEALTH IF WITH ALL THESE YOU CANNOT HAVE 'GOOD HEALTH'. 25|12|89

H. H. & COS 'UNIQUE' SERIES, COPYRIGHT.

75. *An 1889 pun card that is 'Just The Ticket'.*

most collectors believe that the envelope was issued on 6 May 1840, at the same time as the famous Penny Black. William Mulready, RA, designed the envelope (and the wrapper, which had the same drawing), as mentioned in chapter 1 (p. 14).

1884–5 produced an imposing design ($5\frac{1}{4} \times 8\frac{1}{4}$ inches). An additional card, oval, was stuck on as the centre picture; this showed what appeared to be Santa Claus in complete armour reclining on top of a large holly tree. The usual greetings are there, with 'Prime O Meridian' on the base. Various drawings indicate some of the Post Office's activities: a train, Mercury (messenger of the gods), a postman on a camel by the Pyramids, two steam-sailing ships, telegraph and telephone instruments, and in shields the names of four other services: Annuities, Postal Orders, Life Insurance and Savings Bank, with a frame of telephone and cable wires.

The cards were now getting more colourful and pictorial by illustrating some of the Post Office's activities. In 1885 the design ($5\frac{3}{4} \times 8\frac{3}{4}$ inches) had the greeting in the centre of a large circle surrounded by scenes reflecting the

General Post Office: a camp in the Sudan for the British army, a soldier guarding the postal and telegraph service tent, a parcel post horse-drawn van, a ship for ocean-going mail, a sixpenny telegram form, the rural post delivered by pony and trap, a telephone being used in an office and a Royal Mail train.

The 1886–7 card ($5\frac{3}{4} \times 8\frac{3}{4}$ inches) was again historical, the centrepiece being an extensive view of the 1825 GPO building with the Royal Standard on the left and the 1872 building on the right, with the street showing many people and horse-drawn traffic moving in all directions. Above is a medallion of Queen Victoria and underneath an inscription 'Her Majesty's Jubilee'. On the sides are six pictures, all dated 1837, depicting a mounted postboy, a horse-drawn accelerator carrying staff, a Royal Mail coach, a bell man, a rural post office and a packet boat (sails).

The 1887–8 card was even more pictorial. The central greeting from the officers had in the double-lined circle 'Universal Postal Union' and to emphasize international postal co-operation excellently drawn allegorical figures representing America, Europe, Asia,

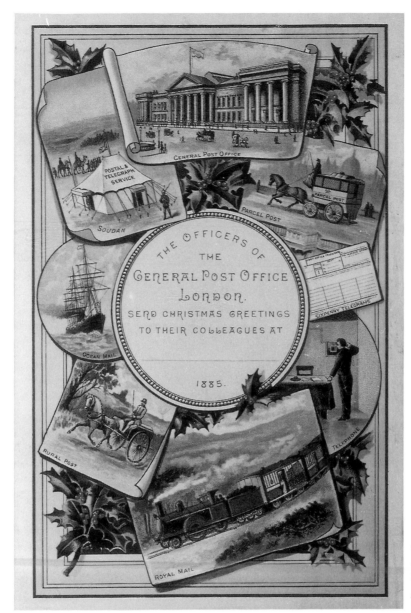

76. *The General Post Office inter-departmental greeting cards are among the most interesting groups relating to official organizations. Like all these Post Office specimens they are expertly printed and, like this 1885 card, show interesting scenes.*

77. *This 1890 Penny Post Jubilee card is the most popular one with most card collectors and postal historians.*

Africa and Australia. Vignettes show mail steamships of Peninsular & Oriental, Cunard, Orient, West Indies & Pacific, Cape.

For the 1888–9 greeting the widowed Queen is framed in a garland of roses, thistles, shamrock and holly. Below her appear Mercury on a façade of a building, allegorical ladies representing Fine Art, Science, Commerce, Agriculture, and on the base Cupid riding on a dolphin.

The originality of these G.P.O. Christmas cards did great credit to the artists responsible. For 1889–90 rail and sea is the theme with a large circle formed by a submarine cable picturing ships from America, Europe, Asia, Australia and Africa sailing round under a blue sky, while in the inner circle five trains move round the greeting. In the four corners neat circular pictures illustrate the seasons: spring, a naked lady attended by two children; summer, a lover and his lass harvesting the grain; autumn, a husband bringing provisions

for his wife and baby; winter, an elderly couple. The message at the top and the bottom tells us 'Day and night by land and sea/The Postal Service never fails.'

The best known of all these cards is that for 1890–91 celebrating the Penny Postage Jubilee at London's Guildhall on 16 May 1890. Twenty six thousand cards were printed by De La Rue & Son; they were issued to raise money for the Rowland Hill Benevolent Fund and were announced in the Post Office Circular

dated 4 November 1890.

'A special card, about 9″ by 5″ in size, containing tinted medallion portraits of Her Majesty the Queen, Patron of the Rowland Hill Memorial and Benevolent Fund, His Royal Highness the Duke of Edinburgh, President of the South Kensington Jubilee Conversazione, Her Royal and Imperial Highness the Duchess of Edinburgh, and the late Sir Rowland Hill, K.C.B., has been prepared. The card also contains sketches of the Guildhall, Jubilee post-

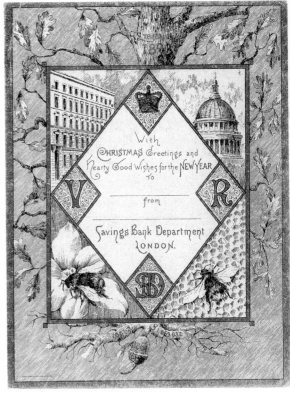

78. *The official cards for the Savings Bank Department are as interesting as those for the GPO. Queen Victoria's reign of 60 years was celebrated by this 1896 Christmas card.*

79. *A well-designed inner card partly covering a large oak tree is one more attractive card for the Savings Bank Department.*

card and envelope, and some other objects of postal interest. A limited number only will be printed.'

The price was sixpence each and over £600 was realized from their sale. Today it is a very scarce card. Unfortunately deceptive reproductions have been made of it, but the Philatelic Traders Society in London was quick to take action against those responsible for the imitations. Anyone buying this card as a genuine item should obtain a written guarantee with it. Is this the only time a Christmas card has been forged?

Other Christmas cards have been issued by the General Post Office, but those just discussed are perhaps the most historically interesting ones for the collector. They are by no means easy to find, for they were not on general sale. However, they do turn up at auctions and some dealers do have an occasional one in stock. A determined hunter will soon track down a specimen or two!

THE SAVINGS BANK

On 19 May 1861 a new Post Office Act was passed granting 'additional facilities for depositing small savings at interest with the security of the Government for the due repayment thereof.'

The idea of a public bank mainly to encourage poorer people to save in a small way, and to enable them to deposit and withdraw money from post offices throughout the country, was the great ambition of William Sikes of Huddersfield. After much hard work, discussions and planning with important Post Office officials and financial experts, his dream became a reality: the Post Office Savings Bank was opened to the public on 16 September 1861. In recognition of his work and enthusiasm, Queen Victoria gave him a knighthood.

So successful was the scheme that within a few months nearly 3,000 post offices in Great Britain were operating the Bank, and within less than a year 92,000 savers had deposited about £750,000 and withdrawn £40,000.

Thirty years on a commemorative Christmas card was produced by the Savings Bank Department in London. The design of this 1891 card shows the Royal Coat of Arms, the dome of St Paul's, telegraph wires, depositors at a counter and a list of all the overseas branches of the P.O.S.B. with the year they opened for business. Printed in light brown from designs by Will Owen and L. B. Raund, the production was by members of the Bank's Book Section.

In the sixtieth year of Queen Victoria's reign, 1896, a large single card was issued (8 × 9⅛ inches) by the Savings Bank Department of London. It shows a photograph of Her Majesty by A. Bassano of Old Bond Street. The Royal Coat of Arms embossed in gold and the message 'With Christmas Greetings and Hearty Good Wishes for the New Year' are surrounded by large roses, a few thistles, shamrocks, holly and mistletoe, with two little angels entwining ivy round the inscription under the Queen's portrait.

Another imposing card has a central design showing in the top corners part of the Savings Bank building and St Paul's. The lower corners have a bee on a large flower and another bee on a honeycomb. The Royal crown, VR and entwined initials SBD touch the centre of each frame-line. An oak tree is in the background and the whole design is enclosed in two gold frames.

The allegorical figure of Thrift is casting doves into the air, while those in flight are carrying messages over the sea to the colonial Savings Banks. A lion stands by Thrift with St Paul's in the background; the Royal Coat of Arms is embossed in gold and underneath this is 'The Controller and the Officers of the Savings Bank Department, London, send

Christmas Greetings to their Colleagues at ... and Hearty Good Wishes for Prosperity in the New Year.'

Yet another large single card has an elaborate frame design with the Royal Arms embossed in gold; vignettes interrupt the left and the right frame-lines with pictures of St Paul's, Big Ben, the Houses of Parliament and boats sailing on the Thames.

Before, during and after World War I the Post Office Savings Bank used to issue Christmas cards, usually with a four-page illustrated inset; these were available to staff.

There were two cards for 1909: one has a red cover and inside the Royal Arms in gold with the dates 1861–1909 and the good wishes also in gold. This issue had an amusing inset and calendar for 1910. The publisher was Juan W. P. Chamberlain of London.

The second one for 1909 is a folded card in green with cartoons illustrating suggested posters for hoardings should the Bank indulge in advertising its services to the public.

The 1910 card was a single, the front showing a pretty girl using a wall telephone. Her message takes up most of the design: 'Hullo! Wishing You a Merry Xmas and a Happy New Year.' An extract from the Controller's Order of May 1910 states: 'As regards the use of the telephone, no doubt they will, now that shyness is wearing off, be used whenever possible.' The back of this card has a number of small drawings illustrating in a humorous vein 'Bank Statistics', such as 'If all the shillings deposited in the P.O.S.B. were arranged endwise they would not quite reach the moon.'

1912: This card reveals in its inset some of the discontent felt by a few workers in the Bank. The coloured cover has a large, smiling Falstaff-type character with a pike standing expectantly under a bunch of mistletoe.

The 1913 card included as an inset Old More S.B. Hieroglyphics for 1914, which carried no indication of an impending war. An attractive cover in black and red pictures a choir of early days trying to sing carols, accompanied by a flute and an early type of guitar; an unhappy dog is howling its disapproval of the noise.

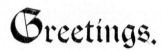

80. *The Post Office Savings Bank cards are now folded, such as this specimen with a four-page inset for 1920, by the artist U. A. Monck.*

The eight-page inset in a red cover depicting Santa Claus for Christmas 1919 hints at separation of the sexes at work due to the increased role of women in business following the end of the war. Other cartoons make this a most interesting booklet-card.

An old-fashioned scene on a black and white card has two elegant ladies and a gentleman outside an inn awaiting the stage coach that is trundling along the snow-covered road. The four-page inset of this 'Savings Bank Christmas number for 1920' has a few excellent humorous drawings and Scott's comforting words 'We'll keep our Christmas merry still.'

For 1921 the cover of the card is dull gold with red lettering, while a circular design in black shows three maidens about to pelt with snowballs a gallant knight in armour approaching on horseback. The eight-page 'Savings Bank Xmas Supplement' contains cartoons with a front cover showing telephonists at work, while the men employees hurry off for tennis, golf and other leisure activities at five o'clock. The girls' thoughts are 'Hitherto we have asked for equal pay: now we must ask for equal play.'

The artist – a brilliant one – who drew the designs for these cards over many years was U. A. Monck. In their restricted way, those produced in the early years of the twentieth century illustrate some of the changes that were being made in the story of the Post Office Savings Bank, revealing the humour, the thoughts and the grumbles of the staff.

The differences in style between the dignified and somewhat pompous Victorian issues and those of George V's reign are very marked. The latter is a most unusual series which had a slightly restricted circulation, even in such a big organization as the P.O.S.B.

But where have all the cards gone now? They were hardly suitable for pasting in family albums, even if the generation of the early 1920s had the leisure or the inclination to do so. Therefore they are probably tucked away in forgotten places awaiting discovery by eager ephemerists, who will count themselves lucky if they find them.

WITH THE POSTMAN'S COMPLIMENTS

Gladly the boy, with Christmas box in hand,
  Throughout the town his devious routes pursues,
And of his master's customers implores
  The yearly mite.

Many years ago it was the accepted practice before and after the festive season for those who delivered goods to householders, or who performed a regular service to the occupier of

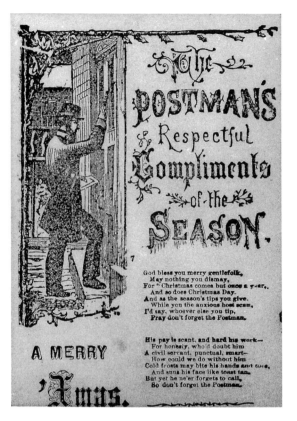

a house or flat, to call and politely suggest that a small gratuity for services rendered would be much appreciated.

There were quite a number of such callers requesting a Christmas Box – the milkman, baker, butcher, grocer, dustman and postman. Sometimes they received a tip, sometimes they didn't.

Today, with but a few exceptions, the delivery boy and his whistle have vanished and most people have to do their own shopping for food. Fortunately, we still have two welcome callers – the milkman and the postman – but

81. *'The Postman's Respectful Compliments of the Season' helped to start off the habit of personal cards of some postmen to their 'customers'. This is a small letter press printed card black on pale mauve pasteboard.*

82. *Three bells and 'Merry Xmas' is the only illustration on this postman's compliments of the season appeal for a tip for Christmas and the New Year.*

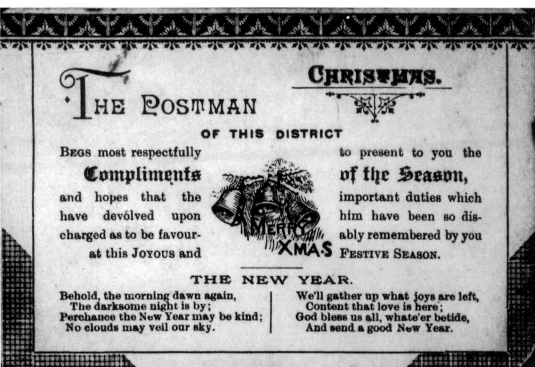

they no longer solicit a gratuity, though there are few people who neglect to give one.

In Victorian times the overworked and underpaid postmen tried to supplement their earnings by a printed card or leaflet left with the mail at residential places a few days before Boxing Day; the money they collected meant toys for the kiddies, stockings and small gifts for other members of the family.

An early example of these 'gentle reminders' was delivered personally by a Mr Cope of Dudley Street, Kidderminster:

CHRISTMAS, 1857

Trusting I have in the past year been to yourself a welcome Messenger of good intelligence, permit me this pleasure of presenting my humble congratulations at the return of this Festive Season, in the fervent hope that it may be to you a

SEASON OF JOY AND GLADNESS!

and that in the ensuing year I may be enabled to give you increased satisfaction in the delivery of your Letters and Papers, to attain which every exertion shall be made by

Your most obedient Servant,

THOMAS COPE,

Postman.

An equally early specimen shows a postman knocking on a door. The ornate lettering reads 'A MERRY 'Xmas. The POSTMAN's Respectful Compliments of the SEASON.' Underneath this are two amusing verses ending in 'But yet he ne'er forgets to call, So don't forget the Postman.' It is a neat card 3 × 4 inches printed black on pale mauve.

Another small card with a fancy border has a central design of three bells with 'MERRY XMAS' and 'THE POSTMAN of this district Begs most respectfully to present to you the COMPLIMENTS OF THE SEASON, and hopes that the important duties which have devolved upon him have been so discharged as to be favourably remembered by you at this Joyous and Festive Season.'

Wm. Griffin, Letter Carrier of Ryde, made sure of getting his appeal across at Christmas 1869 in a big way – $8\frac{1}{2} \times 10\frac{3}{4}$ inches – picturing

83. *Letter Carrier Griffin of Ryde illustrated his long poem with a postman in the snow knocking on the door of a house. A design by Lewis of Portsmouth.*

84. *Canadian Letter Carriers also asked their 'clients' for a few cents as a Christmas box. Here is a gentle reminder to their friends from Toronto's Letter Carriers for 1885.*

85. *For 1888–9 Toronto's Letter Carriers produced a very interesting card to their friends on their 'walk': between the summer and winter pictures is a postage stamp of Queen Victoria.*

a postman standing in the snow and knocking on a door of a house, hoping to get a few coppers from a householder on his 'walk'. This large 'Christmas Piece' was headed 'THE LETTER CARRIER'S RESPECTFUL COMPLIMENTS OF THE SEASON.' Underneath this a 58-line poem pointing out the joys of Christmas: 'It warms the soul and every sense refines, and melts our hearts to read the Postman's lines, Who cheers us yearly with his honest verse, And draws a present from our willing purse, Some slight reward for all his arduous toil, To augment his comforts and his cares beguile...' That 'toil' and 'beguile' do not rhyme would hopefully have been no reason why, when the postman pushed the poem through the letter-box or handed it in with a smile, the door would have been slammed in his face.

Britain's postmen were not alone in delivering their special cards through letter-boxes

and calling the following day to find out the reaction their gentle appeal had provoked. Unfortunately my collection of these overseas cards is not very extensive and there is still some research work to be done on them, especially by other writers. However, there is one country that is often seen in British collections because of family connections with it and that is Canada.

Everyone knows of the very severe winter weather that can descend on North America. The letter carriers, as they were called, often had to battle against atrocious conditions, snow in particular, so there was – and is – plenty of sympathy shown by people towards their gratuity appeal. One kindness we used to see in Scotland during a particularly heavy snow-fall was that when the postman called at a lonely house or cottage he was invited in and given hot tea and a scone, perhaps a mug of broth or a wee tot of toddy, and the man continued his slog in a happier frame of mind. This is a kindness that is also part of Canadians' winter hospitality towards the mailman.

Two cards from Canada that are worthy of special mention were obviously produced professionally, unlike the British examples which have a commendable home-made look. The design for 1885–6, believed to be the first of its kind, shows a lady wearing a bustle posting a letter in a small box attached to a post, a letter carrier delivering mail to a house and a globe turned to North America and the Pacific Ocean surrounded by a stream of letters. The wording on a panel is 'TORONTO LETTER CARRIER'S ANNUAL GREETING TO THEIR FRIENDS EVERYWHERE.'

The 1888–9 specimen, lithographed in colour, shows in the left panel a carrier wearing a tropical helmet mounting stairs with a banner across the top with the word 'SUMMER'; on the right panel a carrier plodding through the snow and a banner worded 'WINTER' above him. The centre piece has a Canadian stamp of Queen Victoria with 'V' on the left, 'R' on the right all enclosed in a crowned circle with the old fashioned message round the circumference 'CHRISTMAS COMES BUT ONCE A YEAR, WHEN IT COMES IT

BRINGS GOOD CHEER', and on either side of the pictures 'A MERRY CHRISTMAS' and 'A HAPPY NEW YEAR' on small cards and below on a floating scroll 'TORONTO LETTER CARRIERS GREETING TO THEIR FRIENDS.' My copies of these cards have the name Walter S. Bayley on them.

Perhaps one of the reasons why these postmen's requests for an annual tip are absent from most collections is that instead of joining the array of cards on the mantelpieces when they were delivered, many of them went straight into the fire, hopefully not before their message had been noted and acted upon.

It is thought that these appeals began in the 1850s and ended in 1909; but why did these interesting cards fade away into nothingness? For the answer we must consult a Post Office Circular dated 23.11.09, Rule 141 (b).

'No other Officers of the Post Office are permitted on any pretext whatever to solicit, or receive, gratuities from the public. This Prohibition applies to Head Postmen and Assistant Head Postmen, and to Postmen in receipt of the full supervising allowances for acting in these capacities... If the rule is broken, it will become a question whether the officer in fault should not be dismissed from the Service.'

Was that really the end of these interesting little cards? They had appeared in the first place mainly because the men wanted to supplement their low wages, for they had a grievance that was justified regarding their pay and working conditions. They received around thirty-four shillings a week in 1896 when they submitted their case for an enquiry, which was presided over by Lord Tweedmouth, when one of the many points raised was the question of Christmas boxes. It was said that each man on an average received £15 a year through the generosity of householders.

Eventually the men were given a slight rise in their wages and that was the reason the Post Office authorities felt that requests for Christmas boxes were unnecessary – and undignified. But many of the men missed the fun of designing their own cards and delivering them to their 'customers' – and receiving a piece of silver for their efforts.

EIGHT

Christmas Postcards

The appearance at the beginning of the twentieth century of Christmas postcards was a welcome innovation for people of limited means. Although the small folded card could cost as little as sixpence, a postcard in bright colours and of bold design could be bought for a penny or twopence.

At the end of the nineteenth century the popularity of elegant greeting cards had more or less reached its peak – though obviously top sales then cannot be compared with the astronomical figures of today. Some manufacturers were finding that very ornate cards were not in such demand as formerly. The labour force required to assemble intricate novelties meant that even with the low wages being paid at the time, the profit margin was becoming something of a worry to a few in the trade.

Austria was the first country to issue postcards, on 1 October 1869. These showed the Austrian Coat of Arms, the wording 'Correspondenz – Karte' and a yellow-imprinted 2 kreuzer stamp bearing the head of Emperor Franz Joseph.

In the *Scotsman* for 17 September 1869 there was a short article suggesting that Britain should issue a 'card post'. So many people had the same idea that eventually the Government took heed and the Postmaster General and the Treasury announced that on 1 October 1870 the United Kingdom would issue halfpenny postcards. But for the words POST CARD, Queen Victoria's features, and a narrow ornamental frame, all printed in mauve, these cards were not pictorial. But two pictorial cards, now rare, made their appearance in 1870. One issued on 1 October was produced by the

86. *This Christmas Greeting postcard of 1870 was printed on the first British ½d postcard which was published by John S. Day of London and is claimed to be the first Christmas postcard issued in colour.*

Loving Christmas Wishes

87. *Boy Jesus feeding animals in the snow. Raphael Tuck.*

Royal Polytechnic Institute, Regent Street, London, with a design printed on the back of the new halfpenny card of a doll and a little spaceman-like figure, with details of a forthcoming entertainment and welcoming the introduction of halfpenny postage by presenting patrons with the first illustrated advertising card.

Even more interesting is a card issued for Christmas 1870; this shows a wide border of holly with mistletoe bearing 'CHRISTMAS GREETINGS' in a panel. The verse in the centre reads:

> When the ruby-eye holly bush gladdens the
> sight,
> And the pearls of the mistletoe sparkle with
> light,
> Think of one whose fond heart with
> affection is beating,
> Who now sends with love this new Postal
> Card greeting.

Printed on the first British halfpenny postcard and published by John S. Day, Savoy Street, London W, it is the first ever Christmas postcard printed in colour; the size is $4\frac{3}{4} \times 3$ inches.

The Post Office kept a tight control on the printing and style of the cards issued to the public, but Raphael Tuck & Son, who fully realized the commercial possibilities if they could produce cards free from the restrictions imposed by the Post Office, particularly regarding designs on cards, planned to break the Post Office's monopoly. Success came in November 1899.

The size of a postcard was agreed: 140×89 mm ($5\frac{1}{2} \times 3\frac{1}{2}$ inches) and this increased area for the picture gave photographers and artists ample scope for their work.

It is no exaggeration to say that the picture postcard was one of the most successful innovations of the opening years of the twentieth century. It became a simple, enjoyable craze that swept the country; young and old, rich and poor indulged in this new hobby.

Postcards were issued for the most important occasions: birthday, Easter, New Year, Christmas, but it is the latter that concerns us here, for these seasonal greetings were the most popu-

lar of all. They appealed to those who were not normally looking for artistic designs or sentimental verses that had to be studied in the shops to find ones appropriate for particular friends and relatives. Selecting such postcards was therefore a quick and simple matter; a dozen would cost less than two shillings (10p) at a stationers – less if purchased from Woolworths where they would have cost only a penny each. They were good value for money and the majority of designs were attractive and served the type of public for whom they were intended.

Cards of a religious nature, especially Nativity scenes, were normally well produced, though in some cases the colours were a little gaudy, but they appealed to those who liked to convey a gentle reminder of their faith. Besides single designs, most of the publishers issued sets of related designs appropriate to the festive season.

Novelties in decorations soon appeared: tiny 'diamonds' (glass), imitation pearls, pressed dried flowers and ferns were used, but the enthusiasm of a few manufacturers began to contravene postal regulations regarding what should not be sent through the post unpro-

88. *A fine head of Father Christmas, a large bell and a house.*

tected. Even Raphael Tuck slipped up when they issued cards in their Christmas series with small tin objects, such as a bronze tin lantern on a tiny open book in 'gold' with 'Good Wishes' embossed on it; these adornments were usually attached to the card by a small piece of coloured ribbon.

Tinsel on cards was eventually forbidden by certain countries on the Continent, for it was thought it could be a slight health hazard to susceptible workers handling such items. The British Post Office was asked to prevent unprotected cards with tinsel on them leaving the country. To overcome this problem, seethrough envelopes were made by some firms to enclose the offending cards, with a small square cut in the top right-hand corner so that the stamp could be cancelled. But this was not good enough and postmasters were asked to treat such mail as undeliverable.

In 1907 cards with the offending tinsel were officially banned, unless mailed in an envelope. Many people who did not appreciate the embargo, or liked to defy authority, took no notice of the restriction to their liberty and very many unprotected 'glitter' cards escaped the eyes of postal sorters. One particular card showed churchgoers tramping through the deep snow and entering a church. Sprayed over the scene was a substance representing frozen snow – a heavy layer of frosting!

Another novelty was the cheque card. This depicted a realistic-looking cheque drawn on, for example, 'The Bank of Sincerity Limited, Friendship Branch', and such wording as 'Pay (space for recipient's name) the sum of One Thousand Wishes Sincere' with '£1,000' in the lower left-hand corner.

Christmas postcards heavily embossed with designs in vivid colours were popular. Often produced by German printers, they had one disadvantage: they were difficult to write on because of the 'wells' created by the deep embossing. However, this problem was sometimes overcome by manufacturers pasting on a second thin card on the back to make it easier for writing.

Raphael Tuck also published embossed (relief) cards, a few early ones being so heavily indented that it was almost impossible to write on the back of them. But there was no trouble with sets such as 'Christmas', 'Oilettes', 'Santa Claus', 'The Glories of Winter' and 'Holly Post Cards'. These are popular with collectors because of their fine designs.

One of the satisfactory aspects of postcard collecting is the strong link it gives between European and American collectors. The only point at which we agree to differ at times is in the name given to the hobby. Many enthusiasts in Britain still believe that what was good enough for their grandparents is still good enough for them so, going back to the days of the 'craze' in the early 1900s, they call themselves simply 'postcard collectors'. However, there are those who like a special term for their own hobby, as do stamp collectors (philatelists) and coin collectors (numismatists), so the word generally accepted is 'cartologists'.

American collectors call themselves 'deltiologists', and Webster's *New International Dictionary* defines deltiology as the hobby of col-

89. *H. Sandford drew this happy scene of a boy and a girl tramping through the snow with a fir tree and holly. Raphael Tuck.*

lecting postcards and explains that the word is made up of the Greek *deltion*, a small writing tablet, diminutive of *deltos*, writing tablet; plus -logy.

Early American postcards were usually printed in Germany, but it was not long before both America and Britain were producing cards equal to the fine productions of the German printers. Excellent embossed cards in good designs, brightly but tastefully coloured, came from firms such as J. W. Strausos of New York City, International Art Publishing Company, Franz Huld Publishing and many others.

Bright Hopes
for Christmas.

I'SE SITTING UP FOR SANTA CLAUS

90. *Mable Lucie Attwell's little boy on the stairs:*
'Bright Hopes for Christmas'.

Novelty types were quite a feature of some New York firms. Huld's Puzzle Series (copyright 1906) consisted of a number of cards in a set which when placed together formed a complete picture. One such instalment set was made up of four separate designs, the idea being for the sender to post them to a friend at close intervals before 25 December, and when all four were eventually received and placed one above the other they formed a pleasing picture in colour of a well-laden Christmas tree.

Looking through an American collection, one realizes how patriotic deltiologists are. Most aspects of the country's history, development, trades, pastimes, sport and famous people are frequently displayed on pages and briefly annotated. Most collectors in the States are genuinely appreciative of the pioneer work done by British and French collectors, and of course they give full credit to the early German printers, many of whom went to live in America and took their printing skills with them.

Many collectors these days specialize in early Christmas postcards, particularly those with impressive designs. This demand for a particular type of card has created something of a shortage of good quality specimens available in shops and at fairs, with a consequent slight rise in prices.

Among the publishers whose issues are sought after are the following:

Birn Brothers Ltd, London. Identified by the letters 'B.B.' as part of the imprint. A number of excellent greetings cards in fine colours, embossed, were printed in Saxony.

Cynicus Publishing Company Ltd, Fife. Martin Anderson, a famous caricaturist, built up this firm with his brilliant sketches on a wide series of postcards. There were many with a Christmas message and like all the cards of this artist they are in some demand by collectors.

Davidson Brothers started up in 1902 as Christmas card publishers. It was claimed that they issued a million cards a month.

Wolff Hagelberg. This German firm came to London in 1885. Its specialities were the chromo-lithographs, embossed greetings cards and the famous hold-to-light sets. This company had to close down at the start of World War I.

International Art Company, established in London in 1909, produced some delightful yuletide cards in the 'Artistique Xmas' sets, one of which shows two cute children on a crescent moon. British manufacture throughout.

Meissner & Buch claimed on their cards that they were in the 'Highest Award Series'. Their fine designs in pastel shades have made them a top priority on many collectors' lists. A rural scene in a wide circular band with 'Christmas Greetings' below is an item to look for. As their

works were in Leipzig (Saxony), this firm was yet another 'Great War' casualty and their London offices had to close.

Misch & Company (1903) used a trademark of three small bells carrying 'M & C' in each bell respectively. Designed in England and printed in Germany, two series worth a search are 'The Yule Star' with 'Best Christmas Wishes', and 'Christmas Post Cards' which includes a 'glossy' (highly glazed) Santa Claus in all his brilliant colours.

Musical Post Card Industry produced a number of cards with a Christmas musical theme.

Philco Publishing Company started specializing in greetings postcards in 1910. 'To Wish You a Merry Christmas', with bells and flowers, is a typical glossy Philco series. With these glossy or highly glazed postcards, collectors should try to avoid those that are cracked or which show corners of the glossy paper peeling off.

Rotary Photographic Company Ltd. The famous 'real photograph' company. By 1902 they were producing a quarter of a million cards a month. One of their most attractive glossy and embossed greetings shows bars of music from Mendelssohn's 'Hark the Herald Angels' with pink roses above and the heads of the five

angelic voices. But when it declares on the back 'This is a Real Photograph', one cannot but wonder how the photographer got the little angels to pose for him!

E. A. Schwerdtfeger & Company produced some fine 'real photographs' in glossy sepia, including a delightful study of a little girl with her basket of Christmas decorations. The period was 1909 when the printing was done at their works in Berlin. At the beginning of World War I the German name on the cards was covered up with designs of flowers so that the large stocks held in London could be sold.

Shamrock & Company (1906). Felix McGlennon of this London firm had trouble with one of his postcards: 'Christmas Day in the Workhouse'. He liked all his products to be of a high standard and as he considered this card to be very poorly printed, he refused to pay the printer and was taken to court where he lost his case.

An earlier postcard of Shamrock & Company depicted a smiling Santa Claus with toys; a very attractive 'glossy' printed in Prussia.

Solomon Brothers Ltd issued a number of greetings cards from 1911. An attractive 'glossy' shows bells above a country snow scene with

91. *Country houses in deep snow by a stream.*

92. *Louis Wain's famous cats in a snowball fight.*

holly and a verse below. This was printed in Austria, but as soon as the embargo on German printed cards came into force the firm was quick to change to local printing, so their imprint read 'Printed at our Fine Art Works in London'.

Angus Thomas was a London novelty card publisher of 1885. In 1898 his firm issued a Christmas card of court size (115 × 89 mm or $4\frac{1}{2}$ × $3\frac{1}{2}$ inches) and according to Anthony Byatt in his book *Picture Postcards and their Publishers*, a specimen postmarked 24 December 1898 shows a finger in a pie and a rhyme beginning 'Sing a Song of 6d, Here's A DAINTY DISH, It bears my Fondest Greet-

ings, and Every Heartfelt Wish.' This is claimed to be the earliest privately printed postcard.

Raphael Tuck & Sons. Raphael Tuch, born in East Prussia in 1821, fled to London with his wife and seven children, having lost all their possessions during the Austrian–Prussian war against Denmark. He started a small furniture and picture-framing business, and from a small depot in Bishopsgate sometimes used a barrow to hawk his goods round the area. The enterprising family soon developed a print publishing concern and in 1871 produced Christmas cards. The family name was eventually changed slightly to Tuck. From that 'h' to 'k' change began one of the most successful fine art card publishing businesses of all time. Queen Victoria conferred the Royal Appointment on the firm in 1893.

The early Christmas postcards of Raphael Tuck are avidly collected today. A few series well worth looking for are: 'Christmas' chromographed in Bavaria, embossed; 'Christmas Postcard' Oilette, an excellent one showing a boy in red carrying a fir tree and a girl in blue holding mistletoe, by the artist H. Sandford; 'Santa Claus' by 'M. B. H.' (M. B. Hewerdine); 'A White World'.

Valentine & Sons Ltd, Dundee. Like Raphael Tuck of England, this famous Scottish firm is one of the very few late-nineteenth century publishers of postcards etc. to have survived. They first produced court-sized postcards in 1895. Four years later the standard size card, $5\frac{1}{2} \times 3\frac{1}{2}$ inches, appeared, followed in 1902 by undivided backs, which gave artists and photographers ample space to do justice to their work. All Valentine's productions were printed at the huge Dundee factories, where each day dozens of machines printed over a ton of Christmas cards.

From 1911 Mabel Lucie Attwell drew a long series of her delightful, comical children for this firm. 'Bright Hopes for Christmas' shows a chubby little lad sitting on the stairs and saying 'I'se sitting up for Santa Claus.'

Wildt & Kray. This firm commenced business in London in 1904. Greeting cards were their main interest, embossed and glossy types being particularly attractive in design and colour.

Early postcards with yuletide greetings have been discussed here to some extent as it was felt that collectors who concentrate solely on Victorian cards might like to consider the chiefly Edwardian Christmas postcards as a side-line to their main collection.

There are many scarce items in this extensive group and researching into their background can be quite rewarding. Not every publisher of this type of greeting has been mentioned, which leaves the newcomer some unexplored avenues to follow.

The Christmas postcard is not a thing of the past; the British Post Office has seen to that. Starting with the set of four stamps to celebrate Christmas 1976, postcards were issued at the same time, each bearing an enlarged reproducion of the stamps. They are known as PHQs (Post Office Headquarters) and are dated with a brief description on the back of each card.

NINE

Christmas Cards in wartime

Peace on Earth, Goodwill Towards Men!

Over the years that message has appeared on many greeting cards; a message of hope through faith, and it is difficult to associate a devastating war among nations with such a message.

How, then, does the Christmas card, messenger of peace, fit into the upheaval that is caused when nation fights nation? The answer is a straightforward one – very well indeed. A few words on the reason why will come later on.

The Boer War of 1899–1902 produced few greeting cards specially designed for the troops in South Africa. Looking through collections of ephemera relating to this war, it appears that it was mostly left to the picture postcard to record dramatic events such as the surrender of the Boers and the dramatic relief of Mafeking.

When Germany invaded Belgium on the night of 3 August 1914, Great Britain, having guaranteed to protect the neutrality of Belgium, immediately declared war on Germany, and so World War I blasted its way into the history books. But our object here is not to dwell on the tragedy of war, but show one aspect of a brighter side that helped temporarily to relieve some of the sadness felt by everyone everywhere, and that 'brighter side' was Christmas.

Those who were deeply involved in the conflict welcomed the one day of peace that often turned bitterness into sobering thoughts, even in some battle areas and on the home front. Except for the occasional raid on both 'sides' and the constant vigilance, Christmas Day for the forces was often a time for opening presents (occasionally food parcels) and cards. Christmas cards and letters became a symbol of hope, sometimes mild laughter at the comic illustrations on cards and nostalgic thoughts at the sight of drawings of the countryside with its cottages and churches, partly covered in snow.

Some of the most treasured relics in a scrap album made up during or just after World War I were the greetings created under far from ideal conditions by some soldiers and sailors. Such items are scarce because few of the amateur artists engaged in combat and far removed from a shop or store had the opportunity to indulge in such activities as creating a Christmas card. One such 'home-made' greeting created in a water-logged trench and now reposing in a family album was from an officer in the Sappers on active service in December 1916. Designed by T. Beaumont, it shows a soldier knee-deep in a water-filled trench gazing at the picture of his beloved and on the other side of the card an officer kissing a girl under the mistletoe and below this Xmas Greetings 7th Division 1916. The paper cover has a cut-out of a Royal Engineers' badge pasted above 'A Christmas Card from The Sappers December 1916. On Active Service.' A staple secured the inset to the cover.

It might not be out of place to suggest that if any readers possess such relics of the 1914–18 war, or come across them either as singles or in an album, they should remember that they are souvenirs once treasured by someone, and they should be preserved as mementoes

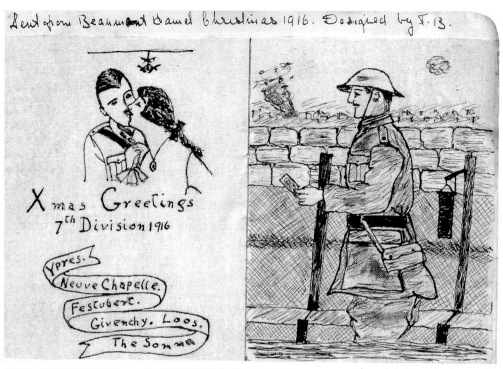

Sent from Beaumont Hamel Christmas 1916. Designed by J. B.

93. *A card designed in the trenches, from The Sappers, 7th Division 1916, with a list of some of their battles.*

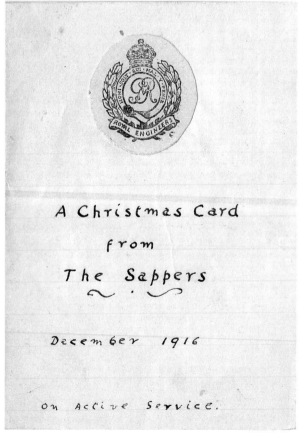

94.(right) *The 1st Battalion Hon Artillery Company's flag, Christmas 1917, New Year 1918.*

Due to 'natural wastage', thousands of 1914-18 cards disappeared in the paper salvage drive during those austerity years. A reminder was put out for general circulation which read:

After the Christmas Season
Collect your paper wrappings,
Your parcels, crackers, comic hats
And other festive trappings.
You'll doubtless guess the reason:
Waste paper makes munitions,
A hundred thousand tons of it,
May thwart the Hun's ambitions.

A number of regiments issued their own greetings, usually professionally printed, such as a large folded card printed on hand-made paper with a design of the flag of the 1st Battalion Hon Artillery Company printed in red, blue and gold with the message 'Wishing you a Merry Christmas and a Happy New Year. Christmas 1917, New Year 1918.' (Posted from France.)

The greeting for 1918 from the same Battalion was a large folded card printed by Waterlow & Sons Ltd, London Wall with the name of the Battalion and its badge in colour with 'Christmas 1918 B.E.F.' enclosed in a yellow border. Inside were humorous Operation Orders, a programme and on the back cover 'Events to Be Remembered' from B.C. 4000 ('No. 1 Pte. Adam paraded in bearskin') to ('1916 Christmas. Hush!'). Happily this was a card to celebrate Armistice Christmas and was sent from France on 30 December 1918.

A short series of postcard-size cards by J. T. Beadle, published in monochrome by James Haworth & Brothers (London 1917-20), show scenes of soldiers writing home or receiving mail from home, so expertly drawn that they have the reality of photography. They are all Christmas cards from the 7th Division who saw active service from Ypres through to the Somme in 1916, and the card for that depicts a soldier in front of a brazier with a letter in his hand and scenes of his thoughts of 'going over the top' and returning home to his wife and his son. (A message on the back of this says, 'I am quite well but a proper MUD-lark

lovingly created during days fast disappearing into clouded memories.

For some months after the commencement of hostilities the sending of greeting cards was banned by the Government for security reasons and to save paper 'essential to the war effort'. Then it was realized that Christmas and other cards were essential as a morale booster for both sender and receiver, so in their wisdom the Government allowed card manufacturers to have a quota of paper for the production of such cards once they realized their propaganda value. Yet in spite of the large quantities printed, they are not all that easy to find today and this is where grandparents might help the enthusiasts in the family wishing to build up a collection of King George V and Queen Mary cards.

95. *Soldiers collecting their mail from home, Italy 1918, 1st Battalion Hon Artillary Company.*

96. *'We always rise to the occasion' is the boast of the 2nd Wessex Royal Field Engineers Company, 1915.*

at present' – a reference to the mire through which he had struggled.)

For 1917 a soldier in a deep trench is writing home and on the right is a list of named battles which has been extended to ten. For 1918 the card from Italy shows the welcome arrival of the mail and the troops standing excitedly around. On the back of this card Beadle has drawn faintly a trooper by a tree, staring out at a hilly scene in the distance, and round the picture is a floating scroll with the names of fourteen battle areas. The sender of this card had added in ink in the last two places where he had fought – Piave and Tagliamento – just before the armistice was signed.

These cards are quite historical since each year they were issued they show the latest campaign in which the 7th Division took part.

EMBROIDERED CARDS

An attractive, though sometimes gaudy, single card of World War I was the silk postcard type, which was embroidered, printed or woven. They came from France (sometimes with 'Fabrication Française' and a maker's name or logo on the reverse), and Belgium. Raphael Tuck also produced these souvenirs, printed in England, in the 'Broderie D'Art' series.

The embroidered ones are quite easy to obtain, prices ranging from £1 to £10 according to the design. They were very popular and most British families with menfolk at 'the Front' received a number of them which they treasured as mementoes of the times when father, sons, boyfriends and girlfriends – the latter in the nursing services – left their homes for overseas to take part in a conflict not of their choosing.

The designs include badges, names of regiments, naval units, flags, flowers, either with a silk envelope pocket into which a small card with a message is inserted, or without the pocket. The woven type are a little more

97. *A silk-embroidered postcard from France containing a 'With Loving Christmas Greetings' on a small card in the envelope.*

98. *A Prisoner-of-War 'home-made' card from VIIB Oflag Germany, Christmas 1944.*

expensive; prices of all varieties vary and the condition of the silk is important. The embossed borders of the card should be clean.

A very interesting and extensive collection can be made of these souvenirs. There is a good guide to prices and types in Stanley Gibbons' current *Postcard Catalogue*.

WORLD WAR II

I said to the man who stood at
   the gate of the year,
'Give me a light that I may
   tread safely into the unknown,'
And he replied,
   'Go out into the darkness, and
Put your hand into the hand of God,
   That shall be to you better than
Light and safer than a known way.'

These noble words by Louise Haskins quoted by His Majesty King George VI during his Empire broadcast at Christmas 1939 appeared on a lovely card with a blue ribbon, published by Valentine & Sons Ltd, showing a lighted lantern beside a tiny print of Mary and Baby Jesus. It makes an appropriate opening to a collection of cards related to World War II.

This is an extensive group worthy of specialized attention, for it covers many aspects of the years from 1939 to 1946, the most dramatic years in modern history.

For those who feel that war and the peace of Christmas is perhaps an anachronism, it should be pointed out that nearly all the cards that appeared during this troubled period had one main objective: to raise the morale of those involved in the conflict, to make them feel proud of their war efforts and to defeat pessimism by concentrating on designs with a hopeful or humorous message. These attitudes to cards were shared by Britain's Allies, particularly the Americans.

Many of the cards for 1939 had four-page inserts for verses and signatures, secured either by cord or tied by a red, white and blue ribbon. Cheerfulness and variety in design and boldness in colour, predominated. In a large collection examined, three publishers stand out: Raphael Tuck, Valentine, J. Arthur Dixon. A note in Raphael Tuck's cards showing fighter planes stated, 'The profits accruing to the publishers from the sale of these cards, will be given to the Comforts Committee to provide and distribute comforts for the R. A. F.'.

An amusing Raphael Tuck card by artist Laurie Tayler depicts a large strutting chicken with a gas mask in a container, peaked cap and a large cigar; the caption below is, 'Some chicken!! Some neck!!!' – a reference to an extract from Winston Churchill's address to the Canadian Parliament in Ottawa: 'The French Government had at their own suggestion solemnly bound themselves with us not to make a separate peace . . . But their generals misled them. When I warned them that Britain would fight on alone, whatever they did, their generals told their Prime Minister and his divided Cabinet: "In three weeks England will have her neck wrung like a chicken." '

Dogs were a favourite subject taking part in home-based activities on cards, such as plane-spotting, the Fire Service and Police Force; black cats, too, were not left out, such as a moggy carrying a load of letters and a huge blue pencil with the caption, 'You can't "Blue Pencil" *my* Greetings.' (Issued 1939.).

The Union Jack made a frequent appearance; one card by Valentines with a red, white and blue silk ribbon, has a large flag with a lion and a crown in front of it with a banner, 'Staunch and True', and underneath, 'To my Boy Friend on Active Service.' The joy felt by sender and receiver of such a card raised the spirits of many lonely young people far away from each other.

While postcards, particularly those of World War I, showed many grim pictures of the aftermath of battles on land, sea and air, tragic scenes seldom, if ever, appeared on Christmas cards. But there is one section that should be mentioned for the sake of recording all groups in the two World Wars and that is the greeting cards that were allowed to be sent home from Prisoner-of-War camps. These are not easy to track down, yet very many were produced for and by prisoners of war.

When British subjects were deported from the Channel Islands during the German occupation of 1940–45 and imprisoned in Europe, quite a few cards were designed, printed and allowed to be sent 'home'. Some of these are illustrated and briefly described in the two volumes of *Islanders Deported* by Roger E. Harris.

A cleverly-drawn card for Christmas 1944 from VIIB Oflag, Germany, depicts a British army prisoner trying to knit a shawl (?) while two kittens play with a ball of wool which has become unravelled and cleverly forms an almost secret message, 'Thisyearnextyearsometime' with the tail of one kitten forming a question mark. For information about other P. O. W. camps which produced Christmas cards it is suggested that the Forces Postal History Society could help with some advice; they issue a newsletter. For the address of the current secretary, see the latest *Year Book and Philatelic Societies Directory* published by The British Philatelic Federation Ltd. For those interested in postal history, printing processes and mail in general, a useful contact is the Reference Library of the National Philatelic Society in London (see *The Phone Book*).

REGIMENTALS

No collection of wartime cards could be considered complete without a few examples of the special greetings that came from the British Regiments. They were extremely well-produced and costly looking, so they give the impression of having been printed before 1939. The pasteboard or paper used is of top quality, the crests on the front of the covers are in fine colour, and if the covers or the inside have a photograph or a drawing in colour of a regiment or a soldier from the past or the present, these were accurately reproduced and are of historical reference value. Where ribbons secure the inset they are of good quality silk in the colours of the regiment portrayed.

Similar cards for the Royal Navy and Royal Air Force also reflect high quality printing.

99. *The imposing Regimental Arms of the Welsh Guards on their Christmas card for 1941.*

When some regiments were amalgamated one would have thought that the pictorial representation of regiments 'taken over' would have disappeared, but this appears not to be so, for, in spite of modernisation and 'streamlining' of the army, the pride and achievement of each regiment lives on.

In a collection of many hundreds of service cards examined it was pleasing to note that, as far as could be ascertained, every regiment in the United Kingdom and the Commonwealth was represented; they make a very colourful and impressive display, giving a brief pictorial record of the fighting forces.

Many other less expensive looking cards were printed for the various services taking an active part in the war effort. Except for those cards exclusive to certain services, a number of greetings with a general service interest were available in shops to the public.

While they cannot be classed as cards, there are quite a few other items that help to build up the story of a wartime Christmas collection. Since it was essential that communication between people at home and the men and women in services overseas should be speeded up, various types of airmails were instituted.

There were wartime single-fold and two-fold airletters with a Christmas greeting and illustrations in colour from some Commonwealth countries, especially the Middle East, also folded cards with 'Greetings from His Majesty's Middle East Forces'. These were placed in window envelopes.

The Airgraph Service (Foreign Section, London) commenced in 1941. For this senders were given an $8\frac{1}{4} \times 11$ inches sheet, illustrated with a Christmas design in the blank area of which a message was written and the completed form handed in at any post office. A miniature photographic negative of the message was made and despatched by airmail. At the destination end a photographic print, 5×4 inches, was made and then delivered to the addressee.

Many greetings airgraphs were produced with amusing designs from 1941 to the end of hostilities. Two books dealing with these airmails are listed in the Bibliography.

An Historic Occasion
T.R.H. Princess Elizabeth & Princess Margaret Rose purchase the first two £1 Savings Certificates.

100. *HRH Princess Elizabeth and Princess Margaret Rose on a National Savings card of World War II.*

NATIONAL SAVINGS

During World War II the National Savings Movement made an immense contribution to the war effort by helping people in Britain to save money. This they were encouraged to do by means of National Savings stamps.

These stamps were stuck in special booklets provided and eventually were either transferred to a Savings Bank (Post Office or Trustee); used to buy National Savings Certificates, or turned into cash again.

To encourage such thrift the National Savings Committee, London, and the Scottish Savings Committee, Edinburgh, issued very attractive greeting cards with spaces for stamps which were freely available to all savers from post office and savings groups. Thirty-five different designs appeared during and just after the war, plus a number without the word 'Greetings'. To form a complete collection of these historic items would be something to be proud of since they are part of the ephemera of the most dramatic period in the modern history of Great Britain. But where does one find them? Certainly not in dealers' shops where one can buy old Christmas cards; the answer may be that they are among the souvenirs saved by people over forty years ago, so all the interested collector has to do is to find an owner willing to part with them. There is no price associated with them – only sentiment.

All the designs are cheerful, some quite beautiful, for a number of artists produced pleasing pictures for such a good cause.

Among the designs were flower studies, children, ships and boats, animals, the Royal Household Cavalry passing Buckingham Palace, a stage-coach in the snow, skating on the ice, Jack-in-the-Box with a robin and holly, religious scenes, flags of all the Allies with a message ending ' . . . when Peace has returned and there is again goodwill among men . . . ', a series of young women in Victorian dress, 'Stable Interior' by George Morland (National Gallery, London), ' The Boyhood of Raleigh' by Sir John Everett Millais (Tate Gallery, London), a photograph of Princess Elizabeth and Princess Margaret Rose purchasing the first two £1 Savings Certificates. A short verse inside by Gerald Massey declares:

Hope on, hope ever!
  After darkest night
Comes, full of loving life,
  The laughing morning.

All the cards were printed in full colour. Sizes vary from $3\frac{3}{4} \times 4\frac{3}{4}$ inches to $3\frac{3}{4} \times 5\frac{3}{4}$ inches so three or four copies could be mounted on an album sheet $9\frac{3}{4} \times 11$ inches to make a most attractive page.

TEN

Collecting by subject and source of supply

Known as Thematics in Britain and Topicals in the USA, this form of collecting has become very popular in philately, deltiology, numismatics (to a limited degree) and greetings card collecting. As applied to these hobbies it means simply collecting to a theme or a topic, such as designs associated with a sport, occupation or pastime. Where cards are concerned it is possible to form a collection of a particular subject running into hundreds of examples, and if the subject is displayed in a manner suggested in the chapter 'The album', the monotony of repetition can be avoided.

Some of the most popular designs are: flowers, animals, children, legends (associated with holly, ivy, mistletoe), robins, Santa Claus, art nouveau and the Nativity scene. Where modern cards are concerned new subjects have emerged, such as space, jet aeroplanes, and in a light-hearted way – particularly in Britain and America – the teddy bear!

A number of pages showing any one of these groups could reveal the diversity of design treatment by various artists, some of whom were famous, many unknown, but nearly all expressing an appreciation of the festive season in their own artistic manner.

While it is possible to get as many as four cards on an album page measuring $9\frac{3}{4}$ inches across by 11 inches deep, a number of small cards showing, say, birds can be accommodated on one page if they are artistically overlapped in montage fashion. Such an arrangement can look quite effective. But if a subject comprising 50 or more cards is to be displayed on sheets, it is best not to overcrowd them, for the various styles of a particular theme should always be clearly shown to advantage.

Jonathan King, who lived in Islington, London, turned his premises into a private museum of cards. It is believed that he had the largest collection in the world. Alas, a large part of his general collection, which was kept in store after his death in 1911, was destroyed in a disastrous fire in 1918 – a great loss to the hobby.

To give some idea of how Jonathan King specialized, he had 12 large volumes packed with cards depicting robins. He considered this bird to be the epitome of Christmas.

There are many simple legends associated with the revered robin: it acquired its red breast when it saw the agony of Jesus about to be crucified; the bird fluttered on to the crown of thorns and tried to pull it away, whereupon a spot of blood from Jesus's brow touched the robin's breast.

Tradition had it that anyone stealing eggs from a robin's nest would live to regret it; a warning that prevented many schoolboys robbing the nests of these trusting little birds.

There are other legends associated with Christmas that form part of the decoration on cards. The most obvious is holly. It is to be seen everywhere during the festive season: in homes, hotels, offices, in fact any place where it can announce to everyone that 25 December is near.

An early appearance of holly and mistletoe was on a rare Charles Goodall card of the 1860s lampooning the bell-shaped crinolines

101. *Santa Claus as Mr Christmas, MP, the successful candidate, by Walter Crane (1875).*

that many women wore in those days. The amusing designs revealed a rear view of three women in crinolines and inspired the caption 'Christmas Bells'.

A number of legends are associated with European holly: in ancient times it was believed in some Christian countries that Christ's crown was plaited from sprigs of this plant and it became known as Christ's Thorn, or the Holy Thorn, in the belief that the berries were red from the sacred blood from the Saviour's brow.

In days gone by in parts of Britain folklore insisted that on twelfth night all foliage that had been cut and taken into the home for decorating purposes should be burnt in the fireplace so that all the little sprites trapped in the leaves could be released up the chimney and allowed to return to the woods. (With so much central heating, and electric and gas fires in homes today, it is difficult to appreciate how

all the foliage could be successfully consigned to the flames!)

A delightful modern black and white card, of limited circulation, worth searching for because of its unusual subject, is entitled 'The Christmas Holly Cart'. It is by a nineteenth-century engraver, Myles Birket Foster, and shows a woman buying holly from a street trader with a large donkey-drawn cart loaded with the evergreen. Boys have stopped in their task of sweeping up the snow to watch the transaction, while two messenger boys are about to pelt each other with snowballs.

More kissing takes place on 25 December than at any other time of the year. This universal salutation, expressing peace and love, is prompted by a piece of mistletoe hung at an advantageous place in many a home and office. In the very dim past it was – so legend has it – as assurance that eventually 'the epiphyte ceased to be an instrument of mischief.' Some would query this assertion.

Mistletoe growing on oak trees was much revered by the Druids, for they believed it had great healing properties; but some clergymen in olden days would not allow it to be taken into their churches in December because, as the Reverend Hilderic Friend quoted in his book *Flowers and Flower Lore*, it was '. . . too largely tainted with heathenism to be a fit ornament for the House of God.'

Yet another legend indicated that the cross was formed from wood cut from a mistletoe tree, and because of its role in the Crucifixion it was reduced in status to a parasite, depending on the oak or the apple tree for its existence. Today this romantic plant is a member of the Christmas decorations trio: holly, ivy and mistletoe.

The other plant deeply associated with Christmas-tide is the ivy. In the language of plants it stands as a symbol of everlasting life, friendship, fidelity and marriage.

SOURCES OF SUPPLY

There are many shops to be found that cater entirely for the collector who is an enthusiast for objects of a bygone age. (Make a friend of the owner!).

In a shop that is really an Aladdin's Cave, the walls and tables cluttered with old books, medals, postcards and many other treasures, one can usually get the owner to unearth a box of old Christmas and New Year cards. Prices will vary from 50 pence each for some simple designs of the 1880s and from £5 to £25 for more elegant, often over-decorative specimens of the same period. Size is not important in roughly deciding what to pay for a desired item; some of the smallest early cards are quite rare; since they are related to the 'visiting card and scrap' of the pre-Christmas card era, they are often prominent in the opening pages of a collection. If a dealer sees that you are a serious collector, he – and more often she – will probably be pleased to make a note of your interests for a future contact.

Second-hand bookshops sometimes have a box of cards tucked away that they would be pleased to let a serious collector rummage through. (It was in such a shop in Fleet Street that I saw a genuine Horsley and De La Rue reprint in an antique frame in a window,

priced £5. This was after the last war when I was trying to get back into journalism. As money was very short at the time I looked at and passed by this treasure for a few days. Then one sunny day I sold an article to a newspaper; a jaunty walk to the shop in question and the frame and its contents in the window were mine. Please forgive this personal incident, but it is related because it proves that 'finds' are made anywhere unexpectedly if you know what you are looking for.)

Quite a few dealers who have an interest in postal history have a small stock of Christmas and New Year cards, also Valentines. However, they are usually in the connoisseur class – both the material and the dealers. But if you require a particular item to enhance your collection you have to swallow hard and pay for it, or bargain with the dealer.

Traders who specialize in the 'golden age' of postcards are a happy hunting ground for Christmas cards and, of course, postcards with a yuletide scene or message, and remember that the latter type is a popular subject so they will not be available at a postcard's lowest price of 5 pence or even 10 pence each.

Among other places to find additions to the collections are the many exhibitions and fairs devoted to stamps and postal history, postcards and ephemera. As there is plenty of competition among the dealers at such venues, prices are apt to be slightly more reasonable than those in shops, but maybe the atmosphere is not as peaceful. Yet some collectors seem to like the excitement of an exhibition where there are traders with interesting stalls.

The big towns are not the only places where exhibitions (with traders) and fairs are held; many small towns and even villages stage such events quite regularly and the atmosphere is more of a family affair. Sometimes at church bazaars a kind parishioner, having searched the house for something for the bookstall, has found some old cards hidden away and has given them for the sale. I once acquired an old scrapbook at a church bazaar and my conscience would not let me pay the low price asked; you cannot take advantage of a dear old lady helper who has no idea of values.

102. *'With Trumpets and with Drums – Mother Christmas Comes'. Very few cards exist of Mother Christmas.*

There are other 'sources' that can prove useful, such as the collectors' columns in *Exchange and Mart* and very occasionally classified advertisements in newspapers.

Auctions are used quite a lot by collectors and executors to dispose of important properties. These sometimes include Christmas cards, Valentines and postcards, but it is a question of getting to know when such sales are taking place and what their contents are. Newspapers such as *The Times* and *The Daily Telegraph* carry announcements of these auctions. All the big auction houses issue catalogues of their sales, such as Phillips, 7 Blenheim Street, London W1Y OAS; Stanley Gibbons Ltd, 399 Strand, London WC2R OLX; Temple Bar Auctions, 128 Popes Lane, Ealing, London; Christie's Robson Lowe, 47 Duke Street, London SW1Y 6QX; Harmers of London, 91 New Bond Street, London W1; N. W. P. Auctions Ltd, West Kirby, Merseyside L48 4EW. Nearly all of these firms charge for their catalogues, but all of these may be consulted in the Library of the National Philatelic Society, London.

Of course the most satisfactory way of building up a collection at little cost is by exchanging with other enthusiasts. In the past Christmas card collectors have been a rather reserved group, but through exhibitions of cards and other treasures of the past organized throughout the country, particularly by the Ephemera Society of London, and press coverage of such events, collectors have come to realize the pleasure of sharing the hobby with others. Although there is at present no special society devoted to the subject, a few postcard and philatelic societies have organized special displays of Christmas cards during the festive season.

The question of firm values for the many types of card has been avoided in this book for this reason: with many more enthusiasts entering the hobby, prices are likely to rise a little for individual groups of cards, and those collectors who enjoy the dignified atmosphere of a hobby that has a sensible commercial outlook do not wish to see that spoilt by inflated prices pushed up by the type of 'investor' who harmed the hobbies of philately and numismatics for a while some years ago. But this is not likely to happen to the hobby of Christmas card collecting.

ELEVEN

Artists

Pioneer collectors in the hobby used to give a lot of attention to the top-class artists responsible for cards of a high quality design. Some of these early collectors were not very enthusiastic about the latest novelties of certain publishers that appeared each year in an effort to tempt those shoppers seeking new ideas in greeting cards.

Frills and lace, animation and comedy were not styles for the serious collector, who thought that even in the limited area of a card it was possible to show the beauty of scenery and the human form.

Towards the end of the nineteenth century newspapers and a few magazines in November and December used to write up the latest Christmas cards that were to appear in the shops, and the tendency of the writers of such reviews was to give more attention to known artists whose designs appealed to the reviewer's – or the Editor's – artistic taste. Today such reviews are hardly possible for the simple reason that thousands of cards for the festive season are issued each year, so the only ones that occasionally receive a little publicity are those of one or two members of the Royal family or some outstanding individual whose card is of some significance because of its news value alone.

These days hardly anyone choosing seasonal greetings looks for designs by a particular artist, but it was very different in times past when caring people favoured not only the work of well known artists but took time to study the verses to see if they were suitable for the person to whom they were to be sent.

A distinguished critic who gave much thought to the work of painters was Gleeson White. For the Christmas of 1894 he wrote an extra number of *The Studio* with the title 'Christmas Cards & Their Chief Designers.' It was an illustrated survey of card designs over many years and writers of the calibre of George Buday have acknowledged their indebtedness to White's researching into the subject, for at the time he compiled his survey a number of the artists mentioned were alive.

Gleeson White was a severe critic. Except for a few of the very early and rare cards, he had little patience for 'popular' cards that he considered to be of low-brow style, Valentines were feeble – he forgot, of course, the romanticism behind them! – and the commonplace greeting such as 'A Happy Xmas' seemed to annoy him: 'It is obvious that for the sake of their literature no collection would be worth making.' In his opinion the period 1878 to 1888 was the happy hunting ground for the collector of good taste, and when we are told that one firm spent in 1882 £7,000 on original work of a few artists it will be appreciated why a number of Royal Academicians turned their thoughts – and brushes – to Christmas cards.

The designs of H. Stacy Marks, RA, were considered to be of a very high standard; a specimen we illustrate is typical of this artist's style. Marcus Ward & Co published a number of his designs in the 1870s. A set of four in the 'pigsty' design sold for 6d each. Issued in 1873 in a size 6 × 4½ inches and in the following year 4 × 3 inches.

Queen Victoria's favourite greeting card artist was Harriett Bennett, who won many cash prizes in competitions for her paintings.

103. *One of Kate Greenaway's delightful studies of children in early nineteenth century dress.*

We illustrate one of her pictures, which has a verse on the back by Rev Frederick Langbridge.

W. F. Yeames, who was also a member of the Royal Academy, helped to bring young women to the fore as delightful subjects on cards. He designed a set in 1881 which was an immediate success; it showed women in long dresses surrounded by cupids. One of the designs depicts the cupids in a large cage discussing the lady in question who is sprawled out in a wicker-basket chair, apparently having fainted (or perhaps she is only asleep?). Raphael Tuck & Son names this set 'Caged Cupids'. The cards are in delicate colours with a gold background. One of the other designs

shows four cupids who give the impression of trying to escape from the too attentive woman.

Alan Ludovici, Jr. who won a few money prizes in competitions run by Hildesheimer and Faulkner, ridiculed in a series of descriptive drawings some of the strange activities of certain men and women. He had a love of the entertainment world and produced some paintings of circus life and dancers.

C. H. Bennett created some of the earliest – now probably some of the rarest – small Christmas cards, which Charles Goodall & Son published in the 1860s. Designs include a man bent double with a giant-size Christmas pudding on his back; a smiling elderly man with a large bow-tie and 'Merry Christmas and a Happy New Year', two boys happily struggling with a big tree in a huge pot, a little cupid filling a wheel-barrow with Christmas pudding, the back view of three women in crinolines looking like large bells, musicians playing in a circular box, and a large Christmas pudding with a man's face and arms holding a knife and fork.

Alice Havers was a prolific artist whose fine work was much sought after by publishers. In the classical style she created 'A Dream of Patience'. Other designs showed elegant women sitting by open windows through which birds have flown in to eat from their hands. Many beautiful religious paintings came from her talented brush.

William Stephen Coleman was a superb painter, much of whose popularity revolved round designs showing young girls seductively dressed – or undressed; but they were all so artistically posed that the Victorians, normally rather prudish, saw only beauty in Coleman's studies of attractive girlhood. The publisher favoured by his work was De La Rue & Co, 1878–85.

Thomas Crane seems to have specialised in flower paintings and Marcus Ward issued a number of square cards with Crane's large, beautifully arranged flowers on a circular background.

Walter Crane, a very clever draughtsman, was trained by his father, Thomas. One of his unusual cards was in the concertina format, on

104. *A Kate Greenaway calendar for 1881 showing 12 little maidens, one for each month in appropriate dress.*

which the four seasons were illustrated by a young couple in appropriate scenes in which the man pays due attention to the young lady; issued by Marcus Ward in 1878. The 'Triumphant Return of Mr Christmas' shows Santa Claus as a successful MP; issued 1875.

Randolph Caldecott was a brilliant self-taught illustrator. Success came to him through his illustrations for Washington Irving's book 'Old Christmas' in 1875. His coloured books for children were an immediate success – he produced two every year. Caldecott was also responsible for many postcards and Christmas cards showing his talent and originality in sporting scenes and pictures that tell a story in a humorous manner.

Kate Greenaway was the greatest artist of her time for pictures of young people dressed in early-nineteenth-century costume. So popular did her illustrations of dresses and coats for little girls become that 'Kate Greenaway' clothes became fashionable for prim little ladies in Victorian society, sometimes to the amusement of other children not well endowed. Kate Greenaway started her career, with a little help from her father (John Greenaway, a skilful wood-engraver) designing Valentines, calendars and Christmas cards; she exhibited at the Royal Academy in 1877. The technical excellence and charm of her work brought requests from publishers for her to illustrate books, almanacs and poems. She produced an immense number of Christmas and New Year cards. Carrol Alton Means of New York supplied George Buday and this writer with some useful lists of the artist's work. As a specialised section of the hobby, building up a collection of Kate Greenaway cards is an exciting and very worthwhile project for those who appreciate the charm and unconscious humour of dignified youth.

—TWELVE—

Modern Artists

Collectors who have a sincere interest in cards illustrating paintings or designs by a particular artist usually choose them from the Victorian period. This is due to the fact that there were so many very fine artists turning their attention to this medium for their work because of the good fees or prizes offered by certain firms, or because it was a 'break' from routine portrait or landscape painting on a large canvas.

Not many collectors have moved out of the nineteenth and into the twentieth century in search of the work of a particular artist. It soon becomes very apparent to the newcomer that Victorian cards are far more plentiful than those of the modern period.

For those who collect by reigns – and there are many who do just that, concentrating chiefly on the social history as reflected in Christmas cards – Queen Victoria's long reign is an immense and intriguing study, for so much development in her 'Sixty Glorious Years' (to quote Anna Neagle's film title in which she played the Queen) took place in fashion, industry, invention and society generally, all reflected on over 50 years of Victorian cards.

The cards of Edward VII (1901–10) are mostly a continuation of the nineteenth-century style, without the very ornamental specimens that had gone out of favour, partly because of labour costs and also a hardening of sentiment.

One artist who has a following among post-card collectors is Louis Wain. He drew a number of designs that appeared as Christmas cards, featuring comic portrayals of his own cat 'Peter the Great'. He was closely associated with *The Illustrated London News* and the *New*

105. *A Louis Wain 'Peter the Great' card, with verses inside by Helen Marion Burnside.*

York Journal. Raphael Tuck was his publisher from about 1890 to 1900. Many of his cards were of the small folded type. One that we illustrate has a short verse by the famous writer of sentiments Helen Marion Burnside.

Wishing you every happiness

Little Mynthurst Farm, Nr Horley, Surrey.

Robert Baden-Powell
Olave Baden-Powell

106. *Lord Baden Powell's personal Christmas greetings.*

'*With Loving Wishes for a*
  Happy Christmas
I know you wish me merry
  All the season through
And so with all my heart, dear
  Here's the same to you.'

Besides many arty drawings on postcards

Raphael Kirchner, an Austrian living in Paris, drew a number of attractive girls for Raphael Tuck during 1900–10, some (monochrome) at the wheel of early cars. In World War I reproductions of his pictures depicting scantily dressed girls joined the pin-ups that temporarily brightened up the wall space around many a soldier's bed.

The well known poster artist John Hassall achieved lasting fame through his humorous sketches, such as the happy man jumping along the sands in 'Skegness is so Bracing'. Raphael Tuck issued some greetings in postcard size (1910) which are in demand by enthusiasts of drawings by The Poster King.

The hard-working King George V (1910–36) and Queen Mary had little time for the gaiety that spilled over from the 'Naughty Nineties' and into the Edwardian scene. The style of many popular cards was still of the 'ribbon and bow' type and to a lesser degree the rather gaudy celluloid variety that seemed to appeal to those whose artistic tastes were not very high. A sobering change came in presentation, for in the fourth year of the new reign the 1914 Great War brought drastic changes in the lives of all people.

In 1920 people were still trying to forget the horrors of war and many artists and cartoonists brought back smiles to saddened faces. George Studdy, President of the London Sketch Club in 1921, whose fat little puppy dog, mischievous Bonzo, scampered into sketches and cartoon films and caused laughter everywhere. This most comic of all dogs was seen frequently on postcards and occasionally Christmas cards.

Another artist of the 1920s with a large following was Mabel Lucie Attwell, whose fame came to her through her wise, chubby-legged children, seen on many postcards and on a few greeting cards.

Lord Baden-Powell, a military genius who founded the Boy Scout Movement, made hundreds of graphic sketches throughout his brilliant career in the Army and later as a traveller. The only example in my collection of this great man's Christmas greeting is a proof of a natural self-posed photograph of Lord Baden-Powell, his wife and family taken in 1917, which I acquired through the family in 1965. He created another Christmas card in 1936, a pen-and-ink sketch showing animals encountered during his travels in Kenya.

With the reign of Edward VIII lasting only a year little change can be noted in designs of greetings for 1936. Plans for new designs for the King and his Coronation came to a sudden halt when the rumours of his personal affairs were substantiated. He abdicated 15 days before Christmas 1936.

A few cards were issued bearing the smiling face of the popular Prince of Wales, and the Christmas issue of *The Bazaar, Exchange & Mart* for 2 December 1930 devoted its cover to the Prince of Wales's card for that year.

The cards of George VI (1936–52) were showing the sophisticated look of the late 1920s and the early 1930s when once again War erupted and began to change the appearance of cards, as shown in Chapter 10. Following the welcomed cards for peace in 1944–45 designs began to get back to normality. With the cards of Queen Elizabeth's reign (1952–) the quality of printing and design have reached a very high standard. There has been a large increase in perfect reproductions of 'Old Masters'; famous paintings of the nineteenth and the twentieth centuries; religious paintings, too, have increased in quality and quantity, particularly from high-class publishers.

There has also been a big increase in reproductions of Victorian cards. These are nearly always excellently printed, but there should be no confusion with the originals, for the reproductions have the title of the design shown and in most cases the name of the publishers.

To 'date' specimens of the last 40 years is not an easy matter, though if a collector has saved up the family cards over the years there will be no problem in dating them, especially if the senders have obligingly marked the years on the cards.

Among the most sought after of modern cards are those of Sir Winston Churchill, whose lovely paintings of landscapes have a vivid strength of character, as one would expect from a man of such amazing ability.

To give a list of most of the modern artists of cards would be too extensive and not all that helpful; better to suggest that anyone interested in the subject should note artists' names on cards received each Christmas and compile a list with the publishers' names. This will help the compiler to select artists that have the most appeal to the collector concerned.

In addition to the paintings of Sir Winston Churchill, a few that are very interesting but are not easy to find include a long series by Sir Brian Cook Batsford, Vice President of the

107. *Sir Brian Batsford's painting of a sitting room of a house in St John's Wood.*

108. *One of the many medal Christmas cards based on sculptures by Paul Vincze.*

Royal Society of Arts. He has produced a painting each year since 1929 for a Christmas card; some of these include View of 14th century Arlington Row, Bibury, Gloucestershire from a water-colour, St John's Wood in the Snow, Incoming Tide and Evening Light from Hayle End, Cornwall and The Garden at Lamb House, Rye, East Sussex. (Lamb House was the home of Henry James, the Anglo-American novelist, from 1897 to 1916. It is now a property of the National Trust). Others include Church Square from Watchbell Street, Rye, Sussex, the Church and Manor, Wyke Champflower, sixteenth-century Chiddingstone Cottages, Kent, in deep snow; the sitting room at 19 Norfolk Road, London NW8 and Winter in Parliament Square.

Paul Vincze, FRBS, of Chelsea achieved fame in the numismatic world through creating beautiful sculptures of medals. After vari-

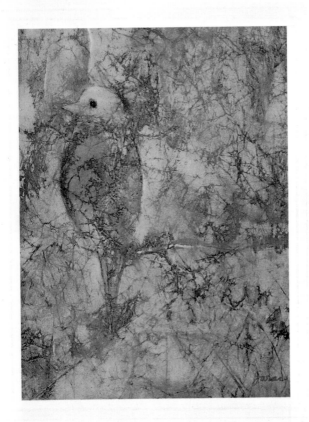

109. *Michael Garady's 'robin' inspired by a poem of Suzette Childeroy Compton.*

Shakespeare Association Congress), commemorating the Centenary of Charles Dickens (1812–1870), a self-portrait and 19 small reproductions of his work, the Shakespeare Birthplace Trust to commemorate the 200th Anniversary of the Stratford Jubilee and His Holiness Pope Paul VI.

In the modern greeting card world it is not very often that you have a personal collaboration between artist and poet, as usually happens in music where composer and lyric writer work together. In 1976 Michael Garady, a brilliant painter of the 'modern' school, teamed up with Suzette Childeroy Compton whose inspired poetry has received favourable attention in literary circles. A number of Michael Garady's futuristic oil paintings with poems by Suzette have been issued in recent years. One magazine writing about this team in an article 'Antiques of the Future' has this to say '. . . so closely are the two art forms intergrated that one can use almost the same words in describing each. Both have an underlying strength which gives a convincing integrity to the surface delicacy . . .'.

A few of the subjects of the painting/poem greeting cards are *Amaranth, Imaginary unfading Flower, Flower In A Mirror* and *Butterfly Clouds*:

Children, come dance to a melody sweet
Unheard in your eggshell hideaways:
Skip, tiny or little or bigger feet
Into the ballroom of the sky . . .
Choosing butterfly clouds as partners
For if they stumble you will not cry.

And *The Robin*:

Robin of the russet-redbreast
Feather-down of earthly brown:
Inquisitive, at times a clown,
Companionable and thrice blest.

ous complicated processes the end result would be a commemorative medal in a chosen metal. Photographs are taken of the actual medal, obverse and reverse, and from these Christmas cards then printed. A few examples include Shakespeare in America (for the International

—THIRTEEN—

The album

In a delightful book *Antiques from the Victorian Home*, Bea Howe wanders with expert eye and a love of Victoriana through a large house of a well-to-do family.

The contents of each room, heavy with furniture and pictures, tables and treasure-filled cabinets, reveal the comfortable family lifestyle of days that seem so quiet and peaceful when compared with modern life.

In Bea Howe's chapter on Parlour Pastimes she states that 'In the centre of the Victorian drawing room or parlour, on a round rosewood table, there usually reposed a handsome book bound in dark morocco leather. This book was the Family Album, much handled and treasured and second only in importance to the household Bible.'

The contents of the album with its tinted pages included, besides short literary contributions from favoured friends, small engravings, drawings, *decalcomanie* (coloured transfers), *cartes de visite* and some scraps of flowers, robins, clasped hands, etc.

Then in the 1860s and '70s a new addition to the album changed its character – the Christmas and New Year cards. These begin to play an important part in Christmas festivities. The Victorians, with their enthusiasm for collecting, welcomed these entirely new additions to their albums; once dignified family heirlooms now becoming scrap books filled with trivialities. But however much the more serious members of a family regretted the change in style of the album, the younger members loved the brightness of the cards and especially the scraps that gave them so much joy when decorating the album.

The author has a number of such family albums which had been treasured possessions in which ephemera of the period was lovingly pasted, building up over a year or more into a reflection of passing events and fashions. From 1870 onwards the appearance was enhanced by the Christmas and New Year cards and Valentines surrounded by gaily coloured scraps. Often the names of the senders and the dates when received were written below these items; this dating is of value to a collector, for it indicates within a year or two when the card was issued.

Sadly, many of these old albums are disposed of when members of a family go their various ways, and dealers who acquire them often break them up and sell the cards and Valentines as separate items.

Good quality albums containing a selection of early cards in fine condition are of value, for they become scarcer every year and, once destroyed, a heritage disappears for ever. Victorian albums can sometimes be bought from booksellers, antique dealers or shops that specialize in 'bygones', also at auctions. Sometimes these albums have had scarce items removed and replaced by less interesting varieties. Providing the substitutes are of the same period not much harm is done. If an album itself is in very poor condition and some of the contents are damaged or missing, then there is no reason why the cards and other items should not be removed. If a card cannot be cut off the page for fear of damaging something on the other side, the whole page – providing that are no delicate Valentines, silk, hand-painted or jewelled cards on it – can be immersed in slightly warm water. This is not as drastic as it might sound. (I have soaked off many hundreds of cards in this manner and had only two or three 'accidents', when a few scraps and tiny flowers detached themselves.) Folded cords or ribbons and white backgrounds should not be put in water; it is best just to prise them off the page gently and not worry about the paper adhering to the back. As the early flat cards were so well printed by German, British and American firms they can stand quite a good soaking if glue rather than paste was used to stick them in the album.

When the page is removed from its bath the cards should peel off quite easily. The picture side should be wiped gently with cotton wool or a soft tissue to remove surplus water and to freshen up the image, then placed face downwards on a sheet of clean, white blotting paper and the backs dabbed with another tissue. All this might seem a lot of work, but it becomes interesting in time, especially when messages and dates are revealed for the first time in perhaps a hundred years.

The cards (and scraps, etc.,) should be allowed to dry off naturally and thoroughly. If any should curl they can be placed between the pages of a large unimportant book and ignored for a couple of days. (The scraps should be saved either for children, or a collector of such ephemera – and there are many).

DISPLAYING

Newcomers to the hobby often ask what is the best way to 'house' a collection once they have decided on the types they want to build up. Just to stash them away in something like a shoebox is no way to treat them; this way, no one, even the owner, derives pleasure from not being able to view them properly – half the fun in any type of a collection is the joy experienced in showing it to others.

There are three recognized methods. First: good quality interleaved stamp album pages $9\frac{3}{4} \times 11$ inches, white or black, which will take from one large to four small cards to a page. Second: plain card cut to the size most convenient for displaying (this would be more expensive than album pages). Third: an album with glassine pockets for extra large cards.

One should beware of certain cheap cover albums with plastic pockets that are not acid free. Albums and single sheets are now coming on the market that are guaranteed to be safe for protecting postal history items, covers, postcards and greeting cards.

Mounting specimens on to pages should present no problems; a narrow strip of folded adhesive paper at top and bottom of the card is all that is necessary to secure a card firmly to a page (avoid plastic tape from a roll, for it is awkward to use). Art shops and some stationers have narrow self-adhesive paper tape which is easy to use and can be peeled off without damaging the back of a card. But perhaps the most successful method to use is the invisible 'photo-corners' that are slipped over the corners of a card, moistened and then pressed on to the page. This of course is not suitable for round or awkwardly shaped cards. With some neat, brief writing-up below or at the side of the cards, such as date of issue and designer (if known), publisher and any special point about the design, the prepared pages are now ready for showing to friends, handing round or putting in display frames at a society meeting or entering in an exhibition, where such a display would cause a lot of attention.

As to storing when not in use, the pages can be kept in loose leaf albums, which will take over 50 pages with cards mounted on them, and they should be kept upright and not laid flat, one on top of the other.

As the collection grows and it is found that it would be expensive to buy albums complete with leaves, you could get the leaves in packets and look around for good second-hand or shop-soiled loose leaf binders; many stamp dealers have a few of these for sale.

A final thought: an acquaintance of mine mounts a few of his favourite cards in old-fashioned frames, half-a-dozen in single frames and a delightful set of twelve of a flower series in a large frame. They have pride of place in his wife's 'sewing room'!

—FOURTEEN—

Collections to see

Within recent years small exhibitions of greeting cards have been put on show by some organizations and firms at Christmas time in London and other towns. They are usually open to the public, but some that are organized by societies and business concerns can be seen only by invitation.

Sometimes these displays, if they are on view for a week or longer, receive limited press coverage and attract considerable interest, for there is seldom any commercial gimmick about these temporary shows, since the material on view is from private collections of serious collectors wishing to spread a little happiness during December's winter days.

In the Victoria and Albert Museum, South Kensington, London, there is quite a large collection of early and some modern Christmas cards, as one would expect in what is claimed to be the world's finest museum of the decorative and fine arts.

The collection ranges from the Cole–Horsley 'first', the William Maw Egley 'second' (the latter presented to the Museum by H. J. Deane), right through the years to the 1960s. A number of sets of pre-1950s were given to the collection by the artists, so besides an abundance of Victorian material, many designs show the work of artists who visualize the message of Christmas in a futuristic or even esoteric way.

There are two proofs of the Cole–Horsley design, one in pale red and one in black, wrongly dated 1845 but later corrected to 1843; also a Raphael Tuck facsimile inscribed 'From John Waddington and his wife'.

Of the rare Egley, there is a pencil sketch which reveals how closely the artist kept to his original idea when making the final drawing for publication.

Many styles of Victorian cards are represented, including a three-panel Valentine type that is so overladen with imitation flowers and ferns that it was sold in a special box for protection.

A good selection of single cards in colour of military personnel shows some of the smart uniforms of the 1880s, while World War II is represented by cards sent to Britain during the German occupation of Belgium, followed by one celebrating the liberation of the Belgians. 'W.E.' was the artist responsible for the humorous and patriotic drawings that appear to have got past the German censor.

The collection is not on display, but is kept in three large print boxes in the Department of Prints and Drawings on the fifth floor. Most of the cards are in wrappers or envelopes, but except for some expertly mounted on die-sunk panels, very few packages bear descriptions. All specimens are lightly stamped on the back 'V & A' and inscribed with a number corresponding to a list in each box.

Mr John Murdoch, Deputy Keeper of the Department of Prints, Drawings, Photographs and Paintings, told me that in principle the collection is available for study on demand to people who call in person to the Print Room, which is open five days a week (not including Fridays or Sundays). The Print Room is very comfortable and informal; no ticket is required, just a signature on a form stating the purpose of the visit.

This is a valuable collection which, if intelligently examined, can tell the student something of the story of the Christmas card. Unfortunately very little of it is mounted on album-type pages or folders, which would enable specimens to be briefly written up. This would protect the cards (some of which can be damaged if riffled) and be of considerable reference value to the student researching the subject.

Admission to the Victoria and Albert Museum is free, but a voluntary donation by a visitor towards the mounting cost of running this magnificent museum is always appreciated.

QUEEN MARY'S COLLECTION

It has been my privilege to examine the large collection of Christmas cards formed by the late Queen Mary. Her Majesty was a very enthusiastic collector of these greeting cards and the many volumes built up from cards sent to her as a child and throughout the years until her death at Marlborough House on 24 March 1953 are an indication of her love of the hobby, revealed in the care that went into the arranging and writing up of treasured souvenirs of a dear family and respected friends.

Except for a large plain album I examined that had countersunk pages, the collection is housed mainly in loose leaf stamp albums, probably given to Her Majesty by King George V, as many of the leaves bear inscriptions in the left margins relating to stamps they once held. (The King, being a dedicated philatelist, transferred certain stamps on to new leaves as he built up the collection.)

The first album is dated 1873–93, and on the first page are four cards; a verse by Francis Davis, surrounded by flowers; this was sent to the Queen at the age of five (1872). The second card has a bouquet of flowers behind which is a greeting; the third has a spray of lilac shaped rather like a cracker, which when pulled shows two hands and silk roses; the fourth, also animated, is a delightful scene of a coach and four, a bridge and sailing boats and a panorama of a town. There is a lovely animated card that when opened causes four separate scenes of people in a ballroom to rise up, and one by

Kate Greenaway entitled 'Going to a Party' with the music by R. Hobson Carroll and words by G. P. Meade; the publisher was Marcus Ward; also a pantomime in four scenes that appear by opening the card (1875). A purse card, that most collectors dream of finding, has an illustration on the front of birds and flowers, the covering of the purse is in green and gold; when opened there is a small wallet containing imitation banknotes, gold and silver coins and a cheque. This gift came from Princess Mary Adelaide and was addressed 'For my dear little May' (1874).

A small calendar for the season 1880 has each page, winter, spring, summer, autumn illustrated with paintings by Kate Greenaway. There is also a dance programme, as used at every Victorian ball. The royal one is dated 1885 and has on the front cover 'Yourself v. Partner' and a small pen attached by ribbon and red sealing wax to a little disc.

A lovely animated card of three dimensions shows two little angels ringing the bells.

The 1881–1910 album has many autographed Christmas and New Year cards given to King George V and Queen Mary by Queen Victoria, King Edward VII, Alex Empress of Russia, Mary Adelaide Duchess of Teck, Francis Duke of Teck. It was noted that when cards have an interesting message or special signatures they are mounted on thick leaves with a square cut out to show the back of the card.

Another greeting from Queen Victoria inscribed 'To dear May Teck' is a large card of birds on a nest with parent birds waiting to feed them. Queen Victoria also sent to Queen May an unusual small calendar (for Christmas 1896) known as a concertina type which has folded sections that extend and show young people in eighteenth-century costume.

One of the many novelty cards in the collection (from the 1893–99 album) is a fan type which when pulled open shows the greeting 'Darling May from Papa 1896. A gladsome season to you.'

An Angus Thomas comic has the greeting 'A Christmas filled with Joy and Love, Your Heart with Gladness Cheer, And may Good

110. *A lover and his lass on the seashore, by Harriet Bennett, Queen Victoria's favourite greeting card artist.*

111. 'Caged Birds' by W. F. Yeames published by
Raphael Tuck in 1881.

COLLECTIONS TO SEE 121

FO(U)R-Tunes wait you through Many a Joyous Year.' Four miniature popular songs were pasted on: 'Home Sweet Home', 'Mistletoe Bough', 'Auld Lang Syne' and 'Royal Country Dances'.

The 1900–08 album is mostly ships, including one S.M.S. Kaiser Friedrick III, sent to Queen Mary by Emperor William II, and a folded card from King Edward VII with a view of The Bridge, York Cottage, Sandringham.

A cheque card Blissville Dec 24 1907: 'The Bank of Blessing Unlimited. Pay to the order of H.R.H. The Princess of Wales, Ten Thousand Joys £10,000' signed Roger Victor Hunt.

The 1909–1916 album is mostly ships at sea; the cards now are reflecting the First World War, such as crested cards from Officers and men of the Army, Navy, Royal Air Force and non-combatant services. One special greeting depicting a ship at full speed in a crowned medallion 'For darling Mama from Bertie', Portsmouth Dec. 2. 1916:

My Darling Mama
May I wish you every Good Wish for Xmas and the coming New Year. I am very sad at not being home this year and I shall miss you very much indeed. But I hope to get home later after David comes back. I suppose you will go to the Cottage again before the end of the month. Best love to you darling Mama.
I remain
Your very devoted son
Bertie (Duke of York)

The 1917–18 album contains many King George V and Queen Mary cards. In particular, one of many from Their Majesties' devoted subjects that must have touched the heart of the Queen: a double card with a photograph, flags and GLESSING. 'On June 24th, 1917, killed in action in France, having served his country well, Private J. P. H. Glessing, eldest son of Mr and Mrs J. Glessing, of Mackay Street, Thames; aged 21 years and 4 months. We have loved him and will not forget him. To our dearly beloved King and Queen, your Majestys faithful and dutiful servants.'

There are many comic postcards in the collection, but one that has become quite famous is a pale blue card of visiting card size, with a grain of rice secured to it and these words. 'The Tiny Inscription On This Little Grain of Rice Conveys To You Our Greetings. To His Royal Highness'

The Prince of Wales
Sincere Christmas Greetings
    From the
Joseph G. G. Gillott Pen Co.,
    London, England.
    Season 1929

Queen Mary's collection is now housed in the British Museum, and may be viewed by appointment through the curator of the Department of Prints and Drawings.

Chronology

1798 Lithography invented by Aloys Senefelder, Bavaria. Flat surface printing from a stone (or metal plate). The Cole–Horsley card printed by this process.

1829 Anniversary card designed by William Harvey, engraved by J. Thompson. 'Anniversarie' appears round a large circle with small figures under each letter.

1830 Twelfth Night. Scraps of characters for a game, available from cake shops and sometimes made into home-made cards. Twelve days after Christmas (Epiphany) all cards should be put away.

1840s Reward cards for children with good Sunday school attendance, widely used in Britain and America.

1840 Postage rates reduced (January). Penny postage throughout the UK.
'Penny Black' postage stamp issued (6 May). William Mulready envelope issued at post offices (6 May).
Richard Doyle's world's first Christmas envelope (December).

1840–50 Christmas decorated sheets (broadsides). Children wrote on these to show parents how their handwriting had progressed.

1841 The Prince Consort Albert popularized the Christmas tree by setting one up at Windsor Castle. German settlers in America brought the custom of the tree and its decoration with them c. 1750.
Charles Drummond of Edinburgh printed Scotland's first New Year card. It shows a laughing face and 'A Guid New Year an' Mony o' Them'.

1843 World's first Christmas card designed by John Callcott Horsley from an idea of Henry Cole. Lithographed.

1848 William Maw Egley produced an etched design: the world's second Christmas card.

1850s–1900 Dean & Son, London. Small animated cards lithographed, and woodcut, hand-coloured. In 1865 large quantities of cards at 1d each.

1850 First American Christmas card: R. H. Pease, Albany, New York. Lithographed design with Santa Claus and dancers, the 'Temple of Fancy'.

1850s Robin redbreast first appeared.

1851 Cassell, Petter & Galpin, London printers, issued the first set of small card designs showing angels and bell-ringers.

1858 Gold printing came into use.

1860 Chromolithography. A separate stone used for each colour. Many stones could be used for one design.

1860s Cards of a visiting card size manufactured with a greeting and scraps added.

1860s 'Father Christmas and His Little Friends'. A six-card concertina set, each picture 4in × 2⅝ in, pen-and-ink drawings, multicoloured. Marcus Ward & Co.

1860s–70s Padded cushion or sachet for powder or perfume; well padded specimens used as pin cushions.

1862 Charles Goodall & Son, London. First publisher of small cards in very large editions.
Christmas decorated notepaper and envelopes (small), die sunk, embossed designs by Charles Goodall.

1863 Alexander Laidlaw, London, publisher of scraps and cut-out flowers.

1864 Twelfth Night characters on chromolithographic scraps produced by A. Laidlaw.

1865 Hughes & Kimber, first used a lithographic press driven by steam.

1866 Lithographic steam press introduced into USA.

1867 Frosting first used.

1868–1900 Kate Greenaway. Her cards, calendars and books showing boys and girls dressed in early nineteenth-century costume made her one of the most famous artists of children.

1870s Japanese style cards became popular. Robert Dudley, active graphic artist for many publishers.

1870 Imitation cheques, banknotes etc in vogue. Great Britain ½d postcard for inland mailing issued 1 October.

1870 First British postcard with 'Christmas Greetings' published by John Day, London, in colour.

1870s–80s Parchment cards, small, handcoloured, by Alfred Gray, London; also pen-and-ink drawings in two colours.
Purse cards containing imitation coins, etc; one in Queen Mary's collection.

1873 Zinc plates used by Louis Prang, USA, for colour as a substitute for lithographic stones.

1874 Louis Prang produced black background cards, followed by red background.

1875–85 Thomas De La Rue & Co, London created cards with a white shiny surface.

1877–90s Hildesheimer & Faulkner, London introduced photogravure.

1878 Bird sounds and other 'squeakers' created by Thomas Goodall.
Eyre & Spottiswoode Ltd, London, Edinburgh, New York, Her Majesty's printers. Name to be found on margin of cards.

1880s Imitation jewels used in a number of designs. Wm. Strain & Sons, Belfast. Cards of ivorine and porcelain.
Silk fringe round cards issued by Raphael Tuck, Marcus Ward, Hildesheimer, Stevens, also Louis Prang, USA.

1880 Mowbray & Co, Oxford. Printed 2,000 copies of 'The Nativity of Our Lord' designed by Wyndham Hughes. Now in London, they still publish religious cards.
William Luks, London; hand coloured photographic cards.
Steel engraved cards by John A. Lowell & Co, Boston, USA.
Silk cord and tassel to secure inset of folded cards.
Alice Havers, an artist of great talent, producing designs for top-class publishers. 'A Dream of Patience' is a famous picture.
Ribbon band and bow enfolding card inset; used into the twentieth century.

1880–90 Aesthetic craze. Designs show peculiar people and their strange antics.

1881 J. C. Horsley designed cards of children for Raphael Tuck.
Canada issued first Christmas cards; design used on a modern stamp.
Cole–Horsley card reprinted by chromolithography by Thomas De La Rue & Co.

1882 George Cruikshank's coaching scenes on silk cards.
New Zealand issued first Christmas card; design used on a modern stamp.

1883 Imitation envelopes as a card design with 'Christmas Day' postmark in circle.

1885 Angus Thomas, London. Comic cards including imitation cheques and banknotes.

1887 Trafalgar Square riot 'Specials' Christmas card produced by Angus Thomas.
Cards for the 50th year of Queen Victoria's accession.

1892 Photogravure cards introduced by Hildesheimer & Faulkner.

1895 Valentine & Sons Ltd, Dundee. Court-sized postcards $4\frac{1}{2}$ in × $3\frac{1}{2}$ in.
Motor cars now appearing on cards.

1898 Pictorial Stationery Co. Ltd., London. 'Platino-Photo' postcard.

1899–1902 The Boer War. A few cards were issued; very scarce.

1899 Raphael Tuck & Sons issued postcards.

1906 First cards by Rust Craft Publishers, Boston, USA. Now a very important group.

1913 Gramophone record cards first produced in America, also in Germany ('Heilige Nacht', 1920), and later on in England.

1918 American 'Hooverised' Christmas greeting card published by Campbell & Co. Also 'economy' roughly printed cards showing how Americans were economising for the war effort.

1920 Hallmark Greeting Card Co, Kansas City, USA. Now the biggest greeting card publisher in America.

1939–45 National Savings Christmas cards in many designs issued during World War II.

1982 Australia's first locally designed and produced cards appeared in 1881. On 15 September 1982 Australia issued stamps depicting three examples of the early cards.

Appendixes

A Printing Techniques

Those who take up the hobby of Christmas card collecting seldom have difficulty in recognizing early greetings. Searching through groups of cards for specimens for the collection newcomers soon get the 'feel' of the Victorian issues. The main reason for this is that the majority of these cards were produced by the chromolithographic process. This form of printing produces very fine pictures with a depth of colour in spite of the flat surface.

Many early cards were – and are still – produced by lithography (surface printing), some of them hand-coloured. But with the great improvement made in colour printing and its employment by the manufacturers of these cards, there is little doubt that this was the principal reason why such greetings became so very popular with all classes of people.

In the Chronology (page 123) the dating of some types of printing and the 'make-up' of cards should help newcomers to the hobby to tell the approximate period when a particular specimen was issued, always remembering that a 'fashion' (or novelty) can last for quite a while; for example 'frosting' which began to appear as a decoration in 1867 has lasted into the twentieth century.

Within recent years a number of publishers have reproduced the designs of some antique cards. If any of these items find their way into a future collectors' market it is unlikely that they will be taken for the genuine article, as most show the characteristic dot design of photogravure. Most publishers state the source of the picture on the back of the cards.

Photogravure is a process frequently used in the manufacture of modern cards. The National Saving Christmas greetings of the 1940s were printed by this method. The process of photogravure involves photographing a design on to a sensitized carbon tissue, which is transferred to a copper plate and etched. The printed part of the design is broken up into tiny dots into which ink is forced. The surface of the plate is wiped clean and the paper pressed into the recessed design. Offset lithography as well as half-tone typography can show this screening effect.

B Societies

Now that the hobby is becoming so popular with many serious collectors, one thing that it needs today is a society looking after the interests of discerning enthusiasts. Postcard collectors have many specialized societies (or clubs) of their own in Britain, America and the Commonwealth and although there is a link between Christmas cards and postcards with a Christmas design, it would appear that no serious attempt has yet been made to form a society of greeting card enthusiasts.

However, one organization is doing noble work in this connection – The Ephemera Society in Britain and in America. Catering for the collector of printed ephemera, the two societies have a great many members with an interest in greeting cards as well as postcards, and through the London based journal *The Ephemerist* the hobby is receiving valuable publicity. In Britain the Society organized a touring exhibition of ephemeral material, with special displays of Christmas and other cards and Valentines from some of the most important collections in the United Kingdom. Non-profit organizations, they can be contacted through the Secretary at 12 Fitzroy Square, London WIP 5HQ and 124 Elm Street, Bennington, Vermont 05201, USA.

Bibliography

Airgraph and V . . . – Mail by White and Mann, J. Stephen, 1944

Airmails 1870–1970 by James Mackay, B. T. Batsford, 1971

Antiques From the Victorian Home by Bea Howe, B. T. Batsford, 1973

Best Wishes, The Story of the Greeting Card by Arthur Blair, Greeting Card & Calendar Association, 1985

Caring for Books and Documents by A. D. Baynes-Cope, British Museum Publications Ltd, 1982

Christmas by William Sansom, Weidenfeld & Nicolson, 1968

Christmas Cards & Their Chief Designers by Gleeson White, *The Studio*, 1894

Christmas Treasury by Sam Elder, Orbis Publishing Ltd, 1985

Compliments of the Season by Ettlinger & Holloway. Penguin Books, 1947

Collect British Postmarks by Dr J. T. Whitney, Longman, 1983

Greetings from Christmas Past by Bevis Hillier, Herbert Press Ltd., 1982

History of the Christmas Card, The by George Buday, Rockliff, 1954

Islanders Deported. German Occupation of the Channel Islands, Parts 1 & 2 by Roger E. Harris, Channel Island Specialist Society, 1980, 1983

Language of Flowers, The Illustrated by Kate Greenaway & Jean Marsh, Holt, Rienhart & Winston, New York, 1978

Philatelic Societies Directory, The British Philatelic Federation Ltd., 1986

Picture Postcard & Its Origins, The by Frank Staff, Lutterworth Press, 1966

Picture Postcards and Their Publishers by Anthony Byatt, Golden Age Postcard Books, 1978

Post, The by Alan James. B. T. Batsford, 1970

Post Dates, A Chronology by Kenneth A. Wood, Van Dahl Publications, Oregon, USA, 1985

Postcard Catalogue by Toni and Valmai Holt, Stanley Gibbons, 1986

Index